D1527782

# RETIREMENT LIVING

# RETIREMENT LIVING

*A Guide to Housing Alternatives*

## Richard Forrest
## Mary Brumby Forrest, L.P.N.

Facts On File
*New York • Oxford*

**Retirement Living: A Guide to Housing Alternatives**

Facts On File, Inc.          Facts On File Limited
460 Park Avenue South   Collins Street
New York NY 10016       Oxford OX4 1XJ
USA                              United Kingdom

Library of Congress Cataloging-in-Publication Data

Forrest, Richard S.
    Retirement living: a guide to housing alternatives
    Richard Forrest, Mary Forrest.
        p.   cm.
    Includes bibliographical references and index.
    ISBN 0-8160-2339-5
        1. Aged—United States—Economic conditions   2. Aged—Housing—
United States.    3. Aged—Long term care—United States.
I. Forrest, Mary B. (Mary Brumby)   II. Title.
HQ1064.U5F623   1991
305.26'0973—dc                                                              90-26863

British CIP data available on request from Facts On File.

Facts On File books are available at special discounts when purchased in bulk quantities for businesses, associations, institutions or sales promotions. Please contact the Special Sales Department of our New York office at 212/683-2244 (dial 800/322-8755 except in NY, AK or HI).

Jacket Design by Catherine Hyman
Composition by the Maple-Vail Book Manufacturing Group
Manufactured by the Maple-Vail Book Manufacturing Group
Printed in the United States of America

10 9 8 7 6 5 4 3 2 1

This book is printed on acid-free paper.

# ACKNOWLEDGMENTS

The authors are completely responsible for all conclusions and opinions in this book unless otherwise specifically stated. However, the range of subject matter is so vast that we were dependent upon countless other individuals and organizations for help and direction. We would like to recognize the following individuals and thank them for their help: Cindy Creyka, National Council on the Aging; Monica Egart, director, Estuary Council of Senior Clubs; Christopher Forrest, M.D.; Katherine Forrest, attorney; Tonya Hart, program director for Adult Day Care Centers; Gerard Helferich, vice president and associate publisher, Gary Krebs, assistant editor; Christopher Kriter, administrator of Life Care facility; Leonard Lieberman Jr., administrator of Life Care facility; Lisa Rafman, National Council on the Aging; Ken Scholen, National Center for Home Equity Conversion; Anne R. Somers, adjunct professor, University of Medicine and Dentistry of New Jersey; Michael Spada, Board and Care owner and administrator.

Several organizations provided information on several topics to such an extent that it is difficult to single out all the individuals involved: American Association of Homes for the Aging, American Association of Retired Persons, Connecticut Department of Aging, Olin Library of Wesleyan University, Shared Housing Resource Center.

# CONTENTS

## PART THREE: DEPENDENT LIVING

# INTRODUCTION

This book is a guide to and exploration of the housing options available to the retired. It is the key to understanding the advantages and disadvantages of the alternatives available in this important area.

The retired cannot be lumped together for the sake of convenient cataloging. Rather, retirement is a time of life divided into its own distinct segments, each of which must be understood and dealt with accordingly. The French refer to our later years as a period of productivity and reward called the "Third Age," as distinct from the "First Age" (schooling) or the "Second Age" (adult activities). Many gerontologists divide our later years into the following periods:

The First-Generation Elderly are the recently retired who are healthy and active enough to live full and independent lives.

The Second-Generation Elderly have begun to experience or to anticipate the debilitating effects of chronic illness. They may still be independent, but they are becoming increasingly aware that at some future time they will need assistance in daily living.

It is this second group that is most apt to consider selling the family home to move to smaller quarters. They have deep concerns about physical safety and desire assistance in routine home maintenance.

The Third-Generation Elderly are those who now require assistance in their daily living. Their physical and/or mental functions have been reduced to the point where they must reside in a protected environment.

Until death intervenes, all of us will move from one stage to the next. At what age changes occur in any individual is as variable as are all the differences in the human condition. We know of octogenarians with the mental clarity of 40-year-olds who are physically active and gainfully employed.

We also know people who are barely eligible for Social Security benefits but who are unable to live independent lives. There is only one absolute in the aging process: if we live long enough, we all will face it.

This book will survey available senior housing alternatives, point out the strengths and weaknesses of each and assess the level of assistance offered. Each part corresponds roughly to the elderly generation it is most primarily designed to serve.

Part One, Independent Living, examines options for the independent elderly. This section analyzes the practicality of remaining in one's primary dwelling, and the steps that can be taken to adapt homes for elderly living. Part One also examines the pros and cons of retirement villages (under several types of ownership) and other housing possibilities for the independent elderly without physical or mental problems that restrict their activity.

Married couples age at different rates. One member of a marriage may be perfectly able, physically and mentally, to continue an independent life; the other member may require outside services to remain in the independent home setting. Aspects of available community services such as adult day care, home health care agencies and other senior citizen organizations helpful in accomplishing this aim will be investigated in this section.

Part Two, Assisted Living, includes an overview of the attractive concept of continuing-care retirement communities (CCRC), congregate housing, house sharing and other alternatives that provide minor assistance to the elderly.

Assisted living is for those who feel that home maintenance and perhaps even basic housekeeping have become burdensome. Individuals opting for these services are either in present need or are anticipating future needs.

Dependent Living, Part Three, examines housing alternatives for those who are unable to manage some activities of daily living without aid.

# WE'RE TALKING ABOUT A LOT OF PEOPLE

In 1990 there were more people in this country over 65 than there were Americans at the time of the Civil War!

The 1860 census tallied 31.4 million Americans, on both sides of the Mason-Dixon Line. In 1990 there were 31.6 million Americans over the age of 65 and 13.2 million of these were over 75.

Those over 65 now comprise 12.2% of the total population, and by the year 2030 that percentage will have doubled.

Contrary to popular belief, this huge jump is not attributable to improvements in medical science, but was primarily caused by improved sanitation, with changes in life-style and diet. Modern water and sewage systems, mundane and unromantic as they may be, did more to extend our lives than all the organ transplants and bypass surgeries combined.

In 1900 the yearly death rate for men and women was nearly identical. With the decline of death in childbirth, the rate of mortality between the sexes rapidly widened. Today the average newborn girl can expect to live 78.3 years, while her male counterpart can expect to survive to the age of 71.5. This difference in life expectancy is an important factor in the consideration of a final housing choice. Any selection by a married couple should be made with the understanding that in all probability the widow will reside there alone for a number of years.

As might be expected, Florida, with 2,101,000 people over 65, has the larger percentage of its residents in that age category (17.8%). California has 3,011,000 people over 65, closely followed by New York with 2,328,000. Pennsylvania's 1,793,000 elderly account for 14.9% of its population, which is tied by Iowa's 14.09% and quickly followed by Rhode Island's 14.7% and West Virginia's 14.3%.

Nearly half of those over 65 will spend some weeks in a skilled nursing home facility. In most instances, the stay will be necessary for stabilization and rehabilitation after an acute-care hospitalization. Only 13% of the elderly will reside in a nursing home for as long as a year, although nearly one-quarter of those over 85 will reside permanently in a skilled nursing home.

# THE NEW ELDERLY ARE DIFFERENT

Those of us who have just retired, or are on the cusp of retirement, differ from our past counterparts. The present group of retirees are the World War II generation. They were born in the 1920s, raised during the Depression of the 1930s, and educated in war or college during the 1940s. They entered the working world and by the early 1950s were raising families.

It was an exuberant, optimistic time for the United States, a period of increasing productivity that raised wages and offered opportunities for advancement. This combination of factors has caused the new elderly to possess certain characteristics to a greater extent than their predecessors. Today's new retirees are:

- better educated
- politically aware
- organized
- financially powerful
- independent
- mobile

The postwar G.I. Bill was the most revolutionary act for higher education since the formation of land grant colleges in the 19th century. For the first time in history, higher education became available to most males in the appropriate age group—and they took advantage of this opportunity.

The booming postwar economy was eager to absorb this influx of new professionals, managers and other workers. Hiring criteria changed as industry and business adapted to this new flow of graduates, and a college degree became almost mandatory for most entry-level management positions. What the G.I. Bill began, new employment requirements perpetuated and the number of men and women pursuing higher education increased geometrically.

The newly retired are politically aware. They have consciously and unconsciously welded themselves into a voting bloc of immense power. This is well known to professional politicans, who take care to treat Social Security with the reverence they know their constituents expect. This political clout was clearly demonstrated by the elderly's reaction to the 1988 catastrophic illness amendment to Medicare. Although this amendment increased medical benefits, it required a surcharge to a small number of the more affluent beneficiaries. The resulting political outcry was so loud that the amendment was repealed in 1989 by a nearly unanimous vote of Congress.

Because of their education and political awareness, the new elderly are far better organized than their past counterparts. The American Association of Retired Persons (AARP) has more than 20 million members—and this membership increases by 32,000 a week! The National Committee to Preserve Social Security and Medicare has more than 4 million members. There are other large senior groups, such as the Gray Panthers, which have local organizations as well as national representation.

The new elderly are financially powerful:

95% of those over 65 are eligible for Social Security benefits, which are indexed to inflation.

25% of those over 65 are eligible for private pension plans in addition to their Social Security benefits.

70% of those over 65 own their own homes, and 80% of those homes are without mortgages.

Combine the above with a sophisticated mix of insurance plans, stir well with a combination of money-market savings, mutual fund purchases and conservative stock portfolios, and you have a group of elderly people who are financially comfortable. They have enough discretionary income to travel, and the capital assets to invest in retirement villages or life-care communities.

Retirement usually brings about a reduction in income, but the years immediately preceding retirement have usually been a time of diminishing major expenses. Children have matured, finished their education and left the nest. Large capital expenditures have been made, and couples often voluntarily begin a financial retrenchment program to prepare for retirement.

The financial solvency of the new elderly is demonstrated by the past decade's increasing trend toward early retirement. Labor participation of those over 65 is now half of what it was in 1950.

This group is more independent than its fathers or grandfathers. Business careers were spent in a booming economy, which meant that they were not necessarily tied to one industry or one benevolent company that might have dominated the town where they lived. In the last half of the 20th century employees, for the first time in history, were able to change jobs and careers without the hovering fear of financial disaster. Their careers spanned an era when the world was dominated by America's economic strength. These factors forged their perceptions and attitudes.

Today's generation of retired is more mobile than its predecessors. These are the people who created suburbia. Their parents lived a lifetime in ethnically oriented neighborhoods located within cities. This generation, with its VA-financed starter homes, moved to the Levittowns and their picture-window counterparts. They left the cities without nostalgia to establish new communities.

They sold these recently purchased homes to buy new and larger houses in another town or state. They made these moves on an average of once every seven years, often at the wishes of their employers.

## THEY AREN'T ALL AFFLUENT

Some of the nation's direst poverty exists within certain elderly groups, particularly those over 75 who live alone on severely limited incomes.

Poverty among elderly Americans is primarily found among older, widowed women and reaches its highest concentration among minorities. The Commonwealth Fund reports that two-thirds of black women over 85 who live alone are poor. The reasons for this poverty are (1) they either did not work in their younger years or worked at low-paying jobs; (2) few have pension incomes; (3) high medical expenses reduced what few assets they had.

The double claws of sexism and racism have taken their toll on those older women, often black, who are either not covered by a spouse's pension or who never married. Southern black women who remained in the South may have cash income similar to their northern counterparts but often have superior housing, due to differences in housing costs in the two regions.

The poor elderly must exist on $100 a week and are often dependent on the Supplemental Security Income Program (SSI).

In an attempt to survey major housing options for the elderly, low-cost alternatives for those on modest and low fixed incomes will also be included.

# AGING

The elderly housing continuum, with its staged movement from independent to dependent living, assumes an individual gradually loses the ability to perform certain activities of daily living (ADLs). Although the variation in such loss is immense, there are certain functions that decrease predictably as we age. When selecting housing alternatives, these aging probabilities should be kept in mind.

## AGING OF THE MIND

There is no major loss of thinking ability that is an integral part of aging, although the ability to react to new situations does seem to lessen. Like other organ systems the brain undergoes some age-dependent changes. Most people over 75 experience minor short-term memory loss. The older brain is more easily affected by environmental insults, which is why the elderly are subject to more confusional states than are younger individuals. The elderly often have more difficulty in learning new tasks and do experience a decrease in the speed with which they can process information. Intelligence remains basically unaffected by aging until the eighth decade or later, and even then the loss is minor. Verbal skills actually improve with age and peak in our sixties.

One of the great fears experienced by the advancing elderly is the loss of mental capacity. In times past this was often called senility, or hardening of the arteries of the brain. Although first described by Alois Alzheimer in 1906, until recently Alzheimer's disease was considered by almost all physicians to describe the onset of premature senility. Further clinical evidence, mostly established through autopsy, has revealed that Alzheimer's disease does in fact occasionally strike those in their fifties or early sixties, but its rate of incidence increases with age.

Alzheimer's disease is of unknown cause and is incurable and difficult to diagnose except through exclusion of other possibilities. Its often slow but steady progression of deterioration is truly frightening since eventually it destroys the personality.

Senile dementia of the Alzheimer's type (SDAT) accounts for nearly half of all dementia, while multi-infarct dementia (MID), resulting from small strokes, is responsible for another 20%. Parkinson's diesease metabolic disorders or other neurological degenerative diseases are the underlying causes of senile dementia in the remaining 30% of individuals with that diagnosis. Part of the insidious nature of these afflictions is their subtle onset combined with progressive deterioration. These conditions can cause a host of safety problems, ranging from fire to dangerous wandering, and families and spouses will often attempt to keep affected individuals at home well past the point of practicality. Those elderly who live alone are at an even greater risk of injury.

While only 5% of those over 65 are affected by dementia, the risk rises significantly after the age of 85, when more than 20% are affected. As we age and approach our eighth decade, this one-in-five probability of dementia must be considered. If we have a living spouse and cooperative children, thought must be given as to how this burden would disrupt their lives. This possibility must also be considered when making any selection of housing for the advanced years.

## AGING OF THE BODY

As we age our reaction time slows and we tire more easily. We have loss of hearing, particularly in the higher tones, less visual acuity, especially at night, and more brittle bones. None of these conditions is devastating. However, in total, and combined with other factors, they make the advanced elderly extremely susceptible to falls. It is not a question of *if* the elderly will fall—it is a matter of when, where and how hard. Every year 35% of those over 75 will fall, and 5% of these falls will result in a fracture. By the age of 80, one in three women and one in six men will have had a hip fracture. This important fact influences the choice of living arrangement and the interior design of the unit.

Even if the fall does not result in damage more extensive than bruising, 40% of the fallen will not be able to get up without aid. Moreover, people over 85 experience four times as many fatal accidents as those between 65 and 74.

Chronic diseases, which can range from rheumatoid arthritis to strokes or a host of other conditions, may or may not be disabling. By the age of 75 most elderly will suffer from one or more chronic conditions. As the chart vividly illustrates, those adults requiring assistance in basic living is infinitesimal in the 45-to-64 age group, but rapidly approaches 40% after the age of 85.

Likelihood of falls and other accidents, the prevalence of chronic conditions and the need for assistance in daily living are all important factors to consider when planning for future living arrangements.

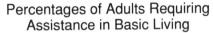

Percentages of Adults Requiring
Assistance in Basic Living

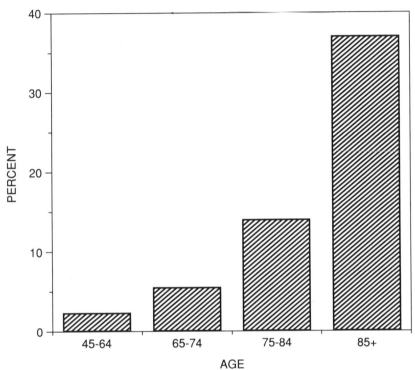

## BEYOND RETIREMENT

The explosive growth in the over-65 age group has changed both the way we perceive ourselves and the manner in which we consider future housing alternatives. Attractive alternatives are available, but rapid growth and often a lack of consumer protections make it imperative to be alert for pitfalls. The wrong choice can be expensive, and, in the case of the frail elderly, can actually increase disease and death.

It is vital that retirees and their families begin to investigate their future housing and health needs and to plan accordingly. A physically active life-style that is appropriate in our sixties will probably not be comfortable in our late seventies. Home maintenance will eventually become cumbersome and driving a car unsafe. Therefore, we need to opt for living arrangements that satisfy our needs while simultaneously maintaining our independence for as long as possible.

This book will help to blaze that path.

# CHAPTER 1

# TWO FAMILIES FACE RETIREMENT:
## The Best Laid Plans . . .

### THE SAGA OF A PRUDENT MAN

Jim Deed laughed and waved the golf club over his head when they presented him with the gold plated putter at his retirement dinner. "This baby sees action tomorrow!"

"You won't be able to stay away from the company for two days," a voice yelled from a front table.

"Wrong!" Jim said. "It's time for the old guard to make room for the new. I've planned my future, and it's a busy one."

As he drove home, Jim reviewed the careful plans he and Doris had prepared. Their financial house was in order. In addition to Social Security, there was the company pension and investment plan, combined with their purchase of tax-exempt municipal bonds. The savings account held sufficient funds for any unforeseen emergency. Not only was the house mortgage paid, but the car, RV and boat were also debt free. Medicare was backed up by a good major medical policy and a long-term care insurance policy in case either of them ever needed a nursing home. They had planned for every possible financial contingency and were satisfied that they would never be a burden on their children.

They had created a calendar of daily activities with the same care. Jim would stay out of his wife's way for at least half a day to give her time to herself or to be with her friends. In good weather he would golf or fish, in bad there were always chores in the cellar workshop. Doris had her bridge club and shopping. Together they would work on the large Victorian house they had so lovingly refurbished—Doris in charge of gardening, Jim busy with its never-ending maintenance. Winters would be a time to head south

9

in the RV or charter flights to the Mediterranean countries they loved. It would be a full and exciting life.

The Deeds' carefully constructed retirement plans worked for three years, four months, and a few days before two events within a three-day period shattered their complacency. Chris Hansen, Jim's golf partner, dropped dead on the course's seventh hole. A few days later, Doris fell down their steep front stairs.

It was obvious to them and their family doctor that Doris's rheumatoid arthritis had advanced to the point where her gardening was difficult and the stairs were dangerous.

Jim converted the downstairs study into a bedroom and gradually began to assume the cooking and shopping chores. He laughed about his new responsibilities and said they were more productive than hitting a silly ball into a tiny hole.

It was Doris's short-term memory loss that disturbed their adult children. It began with minor confusion over days of the week, and even the year. When the forgetfulness reached a point where Doris forgot the names of her grandchildren, Jim became alarmed.

After a careful workup at a geriatric assessment center at a local medical center, a diagnosis was finally made that Doris Deed suffered from senile dementia: Alzheimer's type.

Jim was stunned. Not only was his beloved wife physically impaired by her arthritis, but now she would suffer the slow, progressive mental deterioration caused by this dread affliction.

He read the available literature on Alzheimer's, and pored over the book *The 36-Hour Day* by Nancy L. Mace and Peter V. Rabins (Johns Hopkins University Press, 1981), which discussed the problems of caretaking. He joined the local chapter of the Alzheimer's Association and attended meetings of its support group.

That spring Jim made no attempt to till the ground for Doris's garden, and he sold the boat and RV. Most of his time was now spent on household chores and Doris's care. As time went on she became increasingly unable to perform the most routine self-care tasks for herself.

Their adult children provided as much support as their busy schedules and family responsibilities would permit. Their daughter stayed for days at a time to care for Doris in order to give Jim a respite. In the third summer of his wife's illness, their two sons helped paint the house. That was the July Jim overheard his younger son mutter to his brother, "Sometimes I wish this white elephant would burn down."

It was a shock for Jim to realize that he too had begun to resent the demands made by the rambling house they had once so loved.

The days slipped by, marked only by Doris's continuing deterioration. The nights were filled with her frantic and aimless activity as all sense of time disappeared. Jim's hands began to tremble as he reached the outer edge of exhaustion and frustration. He turned to health care agencies for professional help.

He quickly discovered two facts that shocked him. Benefits for the type of custodial care that Doris required were not provided by Medicare, his major medical nor his long-term care insurance policy. The individuals assigned to the case by the agency seemed either incompetent or poorly trained, and they often simply failed to arrive as scheduled.

Drained emotionally and physically, Jim made the final determination to place Doris in a nursing home. Without any knowledge or preparation, he utilized three criteria for his search: He wanted the most expensive facility available, within driving distance of their home, that possessed a unit specializing in the care of Alzheimer's patients. He found a skilled nursing home facility 40 miles away that satisfied these requirements. Arrangements were made for Doris's admission.

Transfer day was a travesty. When the ambulance arrived, Doris, even in her diminished capacity, sensed the finality of the move. She protested violently and became hysterical. Jim was devastated. As he watched his wife of nearly 50 years being strapped on the gurney he turned away. Guilt and stories concerning the horrors of nursing homes nearly overwhelmed him. But he knew he could not keep her home any longer. He watched as the ambulance slowly pulled away from the house.

Jim Deed wandered the empty rooms of the house they had restored. He automatically noticed small repairs that needed to be made, but found that he didn't care. It didn't seem to matter—the golf, fishing, travel or the grown children, who now had their own lives.

His daily visits to the nursing home were wrenching. It wasn't long before recognition faded from his wife's eyes, and the visits became even more difficult. As his tremors increased he had two small automobile accidents and voluntarily surrendered his driver's license. Arranging transporation became cumbersome. When he was positive Doris didn't recognize him any longer, he stopped visiting.

When the doctor diagnosed Jim's tremors as Parkinson's disease, his depression became acute. He began to question why he continued to live.

# THE WELLMANS' MOVE

Helen and Jake Wellman met at Middlesex High School during their first year of teaching. Helen considered herself a no-nonsense sort of person and a good biology teacher. For reasons she could never fully understand, by that first Christmas vacation she was in love with Jake. He was an English teacher who traveled through life with a naive optimism. Helen knew he was not a practical man, but this somehow made him all the more precious to her.

The home they bought on the G.I. Bill was a modest three-bedroom ranch, just large enough to raise two children. Doris continued teaching, and their combined income allowed them to live a modest, if not money-worry-free, existence.

At the time of their retirement the house was paid for, the children grown and their pension income sufficient to allow them to live a comfortable although frugal life.

Helen was relieved to be free of classroom responsibilities, but it was soon apparent that Jake missed the stimulation. They discovered Elderhostel together and immediately arranged for their first trip. This program, which utilizes college campuses throughout this country and abroad, gives mini-courses in dozens of subjects and areas of interest. The reasonable cost was within their budget.

To Helen's surprise, it was Jake who first obtained the brochures and information concerning a retirement community. "We don't need the house any longer," he explained. "The snow, leaves and weeds are driving me nuts. The new school in town is going to raise taxes again. We need a smaller place with no problems."

"A condo in Florida?" she asked with a smile.

"That's too far away from the kids. I was thinking about one near here. It's time to think of the future."

She laughed. "Jake, we are both 70. We are in our future. Where did all this practicality come from? You were always the one who wanted to leave the Christmas decorations up all year so we wouldn't have to keep getting them out."

He shrugged. "I may be impractical, but not dumb."

They sold their house, bought a retirement condominium and utilized their one-time income tax real estate exemption on the balance of the funds. Jake seemed satisfied . . . for another five years.

"It's time to move again," he announced. "You're the biologist and know that soon we're going to get old."

"Jake, we are 75; that is old."

"I mean really old," he retorted, "We might need help."

"How do I know that you have another idea?" she asked.

He explained the life-care-community concept to her as they drove the 20 miles to Harborview. He told her that for an entrance fee and a monthly payment they could live in a unit similar to their condominium, eat one or more meals a day in the common dining room and have medical help constantly available. Harborview had its own nursing home, and they were guaranteed a bed if they needed one.

When they pulled into the community's drive Helen saw attractive landscaping and campus-style buildings connected to a core containing the dining room, common rooms and medical facilities. The individual units were as attractive as their condo.

Jake suffered a stroke in his 77th year while reading in the community's library. He lost conciousness and slid from his chair onto the floor. Residents telephoned the health center located in the next building. In two minutes a nurse was at Jake's side, an ambulance in five.

Jake stayed in the acute-care hospital for 10 days until his attending physician felt that his condition had stabilized. Helen was able to visit every day, and although they had sold their car six months before because of failing eyesight, she was driven to the hospital in the community's transportation van.

Jake was transferred to the Harborview Nursing Home on the 11th day for further stabilization and rehabilitation. Since he had suffered a right-side stroke, which affects the left side of the body, his speech was unimpaired.

The nursing home transition was not difficult for either Jake as the patient or Helen as a visitor. Located in the same complex as their living unit, it was filled with friends and patients they knew well. The nursing home environment seemed only an extension of their daily routine.

His doctor told Jake that attitude was as important as physical limitations in his recovery. Many patients with his amount of damage were able, through rehabilitation and therapy, to relearn functions and to eventually walk with the aid of a brace and cane. There were variables, but the most important factor was Jake's decision to recover.

Jake was able to retrain his body for many of its lost functions. In 90 days he returned to his living unit to resume life with Helen.

# ANALYSIS

## THE DEEDS

These two case histories have been selected to dramatize certain problems and to highlight alternatives in the elderly housing continuum. Their selection has bypassed a host of other variables. Both couples, for example, have adequate incomes, the Deeds are nearly affluent, and the Wellmans are comfortable. We have also chosen to ignore the fact that in the majority of instances, elderly women outnumber the men, and the widow is apt to be the typical survivor.

Jim Deed was a prudent financial planner. However, he did not apply this same foresight to the inevitability of the changing physical conditions he and his wife would eventually experience. Retirement should be fun. It is a time for travel, fishing and golf—but this is only the early part of the age continuum, which finally leads to a period when physical activities must be curtailed.

The Deeds' house, which they so lovingly maintained, eventually became impractical. Steep stairs are a dangerous invitation for those susceptible to falls. Narrow halls are inhospitable for wheelchairs or those who use walkers. Extensive gardening is satisfying and healthy. It can also be painful for the arthritic. Hard-to-reach cornices and high ceilings may be aesthetically pleasing, but after a certain point in life the use of ladders is dangerous. The housing we occupy prior to retirement or from 65 to 75 may not be practical when physical problems develop later.

Doris Deed did get good medical attention. The determination that she had Alzheimer's disease was not reached easily. She had a full workup at a geriatric assessment center before the final diagnosis was made. Alzheimer's is presently diagnosed by the exclusion of other conditions. A final diagnosis can only be made after death when an autopsy may be performed. There is often a valid fear that hurried physicians will mistakenly diagnose this condition, when in reality the elderly person may have another form of senile dementia, perhaps even one that is treatable and reversible.

When Doris Deed became ill, her husband used everything at his command to care for her at home. This attempt was not only humane, but a valid search for a solution satisfying to both patient and family. Home care for the elderly is promoted not only because of its psychological advantages but because it is more economical than a nursing home. However, if the patient's prognosis is poor, particularly if cognitive functions are deteriorating, home care can become impractical and dangerous. So often with the elderly we find the frail caring for the frail, in which instance neither does well. The available community services are not only expensive and often not covered by any type of insurance, but are fragmented and delivered by poorly trained and unregulated individuals.

Senile dementia can be one of the most difficult afflictions to care for in a home situation. In some cases, the patient may become combative or may wander, a combination that can be an exhausting drain on the strength of the care giver. Faced with this situation, Jim Deed had to face the possibility of an involuntary nursing home placement.

Under the best of circumstances, the decision to place an elderly person in a nursing home is fraught with anxiety and guilt. There are a number of reasons for this:

Because of past scandals in the nursing home industry, horror stories about these establishments abound. Recent media attention to problems in elderly custodial facilities has led some to somewhat unfairly condemn all nursing homes. Skilled nursing homes are a highly regulated industry, while custodial facilities often are not.

It is difficult for the uninitiated to tell the difference between good nursing homes and bad ones.

The decision for nursing home placement is often the selection of that individual's last domicile. This note of finality often translates into a perceived sentence of death.

The concerned relative asks, "Why couldn't I have done more?" There is no answer to a guilt-ridden question of that nature except the necessity for a mature acceptance that everything possible and practical has been done.

Jim Deed was not in an emotional state to make a rational and prudent decision concerning his wife's placement. His assumption that the highest price buys the best care was not valid. His selection of a facility with an Alzheimer's unit was an excellent choice.

The day of Helen Deed's transfer to the nursing home was a disaster. Obviously, no preparation had been made to orient her to this change, nor was an attempt made to transport her in a less traumatic manner. The effects of this turmoil impaired her ability to adjust to the facility and made her a prime candidate for life-threatening health problems.

It was not unusual for Jim Deed to entertain thoughts of killing himself. The suicide rate for elderly males, particularly widowers or those separated, is triple that of other age groups. Substance abuse is also widespread. It is a possible course of behavior that should be watched for in any elderly male who has become extremely depressed.


## THE WELLMANS

Jake Wellman, for all his daydreaming, had a concept of aging. At the appropriate junctures in their life, he not only suggested, but took positive action toward, changes in their housing arrangements.

It is possible that their first move, from the house to a smaller condo, was instigated because of Jake's dislike of home maintenance chores, but it also was a practical choice at that stage of their lives. Their move to a life-care community solved potential future problems that the Deeds, in contrast, were forced to face.

Life-care communities are an attractive concept because they provide medical facilities and a nursing home, usually at the same location. Thus, any transfer to the nursing home is not fraught with guilt for the family or traumatizing to the patient. Moving into a nursing home bed becomes merely a lateral transfer within the same community.

The congregate living arrangements provided by these communities can be utilized as needed. Transportation vans are available for those who do not drive and, in many instances, the projects are self-contained for most services. The monthly payments usually include at least one meal a day in the dining room, with other meals or tray service available at reasonable additional cost. A great many potential problems for the advanced elderly can be avoided by choosing this life-style.

# PLANNING IS MORE THAN MONEY

Prudent financial planning is not the panacea for retirement living. As we age, we must throw off the young's delusions of immortality. A prudent, moderate life-style is an obvious necessity, but even with this care, we will all eventually experience the physical changes of aging.

It is how we adapt to these changes that determines where and how we live. Rather than restructure our living quarters that are no longer appropriate, we must consider a move to a more fitting environment.

While one history illustrated a life-care community as an attractive alternative, it did not indicate the problems the average person faces when choosing such an arrangement. There are problems with life care, just as there are in the regulated nursing home industry. The first step is the realization that entering the elderly housing continuum may be a necessity, the second is learning how to make the proper selection.

———— PART ONE ————

# INDEPENDENT
# LIVING

The ability to live independently is not tied to age. You may be recently retired, or 90; but to be independent you must be mentally alert and able to care for yourself in all areas of life's daily necessities.

This life-style is not restricted to those who still play smashing games of tennis or 18 holes of golf without a cart. It also includes those who ambulate with walkers, those who have restricted many of their past activities and those who wheel themselves in wheelchairs. Independence assumes that an individual can still drive a car or use public transportation. Independence also requires that routine household chores can still be accomplished and that dressing, grooming, cooking and other self-care tasks can be done without outside assistance.

While the independent elderly may delegate heavy chores, such as grass mowing or snow shoveling, to others, they are still able to enjoy outside activities such as restaurants, travel or trips to the local senior center.

While the independent elderly may still participate in climbing mountains (well, low mountains), they may also have some of their past strenuous activities restricted by the beginnings of chronic illness or simply the careful husbanding of energy. The thoughtful may circumscribe certain activities out of a prudent fear of falls and other accidents. However, they are still able to operate within society basically on their own terms.

The progression of married couples through the health continuum will not be evenly matched. One spouse or the other may suffer an acute or chronic disability. Certain sections of Part One will consider this possibility. It is entirely possible that one member of the couple is unable to live independently without massive aid from the other. This possibility will also be examined.

# CHAPTER 2

# STAYING PUT: Living Out Your Life in the Old Homestead

## MEMORIES—AND MORTGAGE-FREE

The authors, parents of six, still have memories of a day long ago when a four-year-old boy danced sideways from the kitchen as young children are wont to do. His smaller sister, not to be outdone, danced on the radiator cover with a smiling plea to be noticed. These memories, caught in the web of time, remain vivid, while today a physician and lawyer pretend to be the mature versions of those children. We, of course, know differently, and forever will remember the fawn-like prance of the boy and the exuberant energy of the little girl.

Moments in time frozen and forever held. It is from such slender strands that memories weave their tenacious grip.

Those things happened in a nine-room Dutch Colonial purchased in the early 1960s with a low down payment and a VA mortgage. The purchase price of $24,000 cost $190 a month to carry, including property taxes and insurance. In 1990, the mortgage on that house is paid and the market value is now $285,000. However, the real estate taxes now exceed the past mortgage payments by one-third. Home fuel oil, which averaged 18¢ a gallon at the time of purchase, now usually exceeds $1.00 a gallon in this New England market.

The increases in utilities and taxes still make this large home the most reasonable housing alternative on financial grounds. This house is now a home filled with memories and room enough for children and grandchildren to visit comfortably.

A housing budget that is within a retirement income, a host of benign ghosts peopling the premises and enough room to store the accumulation of

18

a lifetime would seem to argue persuasively for remaining. And yet, there are matters that require reflection.

It snows in New England. In revenge for this onslaught, spring brings a renewed growth of dandelions that seem intent on capturing the yard. The grass proliferates and requires weekly mowing. The washer and dryer are in the basement of this three-story house, while the study with adjacent bath is on the third floor. As in many suburban communities, "mass transportation" consists of an unused railway line whose station is now a trendy restaurant, and a commuter bus that leaves at 8:07 in the morning and returns at 5:42 in the afternoon. An automobile and the ability to drive one are not luxuries, but instruments of survival.

The thousand-percent appreciation of the real estate value is pleasant to contemplate, but meaningless unless the property is sold.

# WHY MOVE?

Although the list of plus and minus factors is long, the prime criteria concerning disposal or retention of the family manse are:

· health
· finances
· social factors

If an elderly individual or couple are infirm to the point where living in a given house or apartment is dangerous, then the choice is obvious. Just as elementary are the financial factors that may encourage the sale of a home. The proximity of friends or relatives in the neighborhood can also be an overriding consideration for remaining.

The points mentioned above can sway people in either direction, completely dependent on the subjective evaluation of the individual or couple involved. There is, however, one prime factor that must be clearly understood in making the determination whether to sell or retain a free-standing home. The individual house reserves the greatest amount of personal freedom, and therefore control, to the occupants.

The most benign retirement community has certain rules and restrictions for its residents. While local ordinances may not allow the single-family home owner to raise hogs in the front yard, the retirement community may restrict the size of pets, the type of clothesline and even the exterior color of the dwelling. Condominium or cooperative ownership subjects the participants to rule by committee. Other types of occupancy, because they have certain group living aspects, are restricted to greater or lesser degrees. For some, these restrictions are so minimal as to not affect their lives in any respect. For rugged individualists, any restrictions at all may smack of totalitarianism.

## Advantages and Disadvantages of Staying in Your Home

| Advantages | Disadvantages |
| --- | --- |
| No need to adjust to new friends and areas. | If adjustments are ever to be necessary, it may be easier to make them now. |
| The mortgage is all or mostly paid. | It would be pleasant to enjoy some of the home equity we have accumulated. |
| We can obtain a RAM (Reverse Annuity Mortgage) to get some of our equity from the house. | A RAM depletes our estate. |
| There's plenty of room for the kids to visit. | Two bedrooms would still allow room for visitors. |
| The recreation room is great for the grandchildren to use. | A retirement village has pools, game rooms, even golf and tennis. |
| Our friends are all here. | Our friends have all moved. |
| The state and town offer tax relief for senior citizens. | Increasing school costs are driving up property rates. |
| It's a great neighborhood. | It's a lousy neighborhood. |
| It's a stable neighborhood. | All the new people have kids, and we trip over bikes and skates. |
| We can't bear to leave any of our things. | We need to get rid of some of this junk. |
| We need the storage space. | Junk accumulates in direct proportion to the amount of storage space available. |
| We know to the penny the cost of running the house. | The costs of running a large house are astronomical. |
| We are used to the facilities like shopping, churches, movies and town services. | The neighborhood has gone downhill recently. |
| We feel safe here. | We are scared to death here. |

| Advantages | Disadvantages |
|---|---|
| Moving would mean leaving our church, club and social groups. | We aren't interested in a frantic round of activities anymore. |
| We want to leave the house to the children. | The kids aren't interested in the house, and they have their own lives now. |
| The house is finally exactly the way we want it. | Home maintenance is killing us, particularly mowing and shoveling. |
| The house is easy to heat and run. | Oil and utility charges are eating up our budget. |
| We love to garden. | It's getting difficult to do all that stooping and weeding. |
| We can hire people for the heavy chores. | We can't get anyone to work anymore. The neighborhood kids are grown, and we can't afford professional rates. |
| We love our pets. | A cat or bird can go anywhere. |
| We can do as we please in our home. | Community living does have rules, but they are for everyone's benefit. |
| We have a basement workshop and sewing room. | Many retirement villages have activity rooms in their common areas. |
| We can always sell the house if we have to. | A distress sale is disastrous to a real estate price. |
| We will stay as long as we can because we love it here. | Decisions should be made well in advance, as emergency moves may be ill-considered. |
| We'll go to one of those damn nursing homes the day after we have to. | The really good and affordable nursing homes have long waiting lists. |
| Our car takes us anywhere. | The day will arrive when we can't drive. |
| There's always public transportation. | There isn't any convenient public transportation nearby. |

**Advantages and Disadvantages of Staying in Your Home (cont.)**

| Advantages | Disadvantages |
| --- | --- |
| If my spouse should die, I want his or her memories to surround me as they would in this house. | If my spouse should die, this house would haunt me. |
| If one of us should become ill, we will build wheelchair ramps, and make other necessary changes that might be needed. | If one of us should become ill, the narrow halls, steep steps, and location would make staying here impossible. |
| We enjoy the four seasons of the year. | We have seen our last snowflake. |
| 911 brings all the emergency help we need. | We're isolated here; if anything happened . . . |
| If we need nursing or homemaker help, we'll get it. | We can't depend on or afford to hire people to come in. |

# DON'T IGNORE THE STATS

So, you have decided to stay. After this decision has been made, the most important consideration is planning for your future needs and limitations. Certain changes in your life-style must be anticipated so that arrangements can be made prior to accidents or disabilities. Failure to recognize what the future holds, ignoring the march of age with its gradual loss of function, will only increase the severity of problems when they do occur.

We know that as we age, and move to the next level of retirement, there will be loss of visual acuity, general strength, energy, and . . .

### BY THE AGE OF 75—

20% of us will need some help with our ADLs (Activities of Daily Living, which include personal grooming, bathing, eating, dressing, toileting, walking, shopping and preparing meals).

35% of us will fall each year, and almost half of us will not be able to get up without assistance.

More than half of us will suffer from one or more chronic diseases or conditions.

### BY THE AGE OF 80—

One in three women and one in six men will have broken a hip.

**BY THE AGE OF 85—**

Nearly half of us will need help with our ADLs.
20% (or more) will have developed Alzheimer's disease.
40% of the males and 30% of the females will have suffered a stroke.

# PLAYING IT SAFE

The statistics inform us that we are going to lose function as we age. Another batch of figures, tied to this loss of certain abilities, indicates how prone to accidents the elderly are. Falls, for example, are the leading cause of accidental death for people over 75. Seventy percent of all fatal falls in the United States involve people over 65. Almost all these falls occur in the home.

A few prudent steps can radically reduce the risk of accident and make life easier as we age at home.

At an earlier point in time you may have baby-proofed your home. Caustic substances were put out of reach, steep stairs were protected by accordion gates, breakable objects were placed out of reach and other danger areas were sealed off from toddlers. Now is the time to take the same prudent care of the house for youself. Modify your home with a few simple safeguards that will reduce accidents and help you maintain your independence.

# MODIFYING YOUR HOUSE OR APARTMENT

A few of the suggestions listed below might prove expensive to install in an older home. Most of the suggestions can be installed at little cost. Hopefully, major renovations, such as installation of circuit breakers, etc., might be done while the individual is still employed but anticipating retirement.

### EXTERIOR

Beware of rodents and other animals that dig holes that trip people.

Keep track of lawn tools; a forgotten rake in the grass is an accident waiting to happen.

A low fence or branch may have been there for years, but one day you just aren't going to see it.

Sell or give away all ladders.

Watch out for neighborhood children who leave toys in the yard or on the walk. Seventy is a poor time to take up skateboarding.

Walks and exterior stairs should be well lit.

All steps must have handrails.

Do not clean gutters, fix roofs or climb to other high places.

Have exterior lights that can be activated by the occupant of a car or that automatically turn on after dark.

## HALLS AND STAIRS

All carpeting and runners must be carefully secured. All carpeting should be low pile.

All steps must have sturdy banisters or handrails, including attic and cellar stairs. Mark the last step.

Standard doors are 32 inches wide; 36 inches is necessary to allow wheelchairs and walkers to pass comfortably.

Nonskid strips should be fixed to uncarpeted stairs.

Floorboards and stairs should be in good repair.

Avoid waxed floors.

## LIGHTING AND WIRING

Fluorescent lights that flicker cause headaches and perhaps disorientation in some elderly.

As we age, we require a great deal more light, but are also susceptible to glare. Use "daylight" light bulbs.

Night lights should be used in the bedroom, bath and hallways.

A flashlight should be kept near the bed.

Install lights under cabinets and in shadowy areas throughout the house.

Old-fashioned fuse boxes should be replaced with circuit breakers.

Replace light switches with toggles that glow in the dark.

Discard frayed extension cords, which can cause shock as well as trip you.

Floor lamps fall easily—replace them.

*If possible,* electrical outlets should be 18 inches from the floor to be more accessible.

## KITCHENS

Floors should be of a nonskid material. Indoor/outdoor-type kitchen carpeting is recommended.

Poisonous or noxious substances should be stored well away from food so that they are not confused.

Set your hot-water heater at 110 degrees to prevent accidental burning in the kitchen or bath, or install anti-scald mechanisms.

Do not use high shelves that require ladder-steps or any other such device.

Have a smoke detector and fire extinguisher in the room.

Use an oven timer when baking.

Use a wind-up timer when cooking on top of stove.

Boil water in a whistling teapot.

Lower kitchen cabinets from the standard 24 inches to 15 inches above the counter.

Install a built-in wall oven at eye level.

If gas is used for cooking, buy a gas-sniffer alarm.

## BATHROOMS

Install grab bars near the toilet and in the shower or tub.

The shower or tub should have a nonskid mat.

Install hand showers in the tub or shower.

A portable chair with a back and rubber feet helps unsteady people in the shower.

To insure proper use and care, prescription medications should be kept in a kitchen cabinet that is removed from heat sources. Large labels with the prescription instructions should be affixed to the container, or better yet, use a seven-day pill organizer.

Add an extender to raise the toilet seat if you find the standard height difficult.

Hang a vertical mirror in the bathroom, and raise the vanity to 36 inches instead of the standard 32.

If possible, install a barrier-free bathtub and shower.

## FURNITURE

One of the great dangers of falling is hitting the sharp edge of a coffee table or similar piece of furniture. If possible, nearly all furniture should have rounded edges.

Sofas and easy chairs usually have seats of 23 to 25 inches or more deep. A 20-inch seat gives excellent support and makes rising far easier.

A house filled with small tables, a thousand knickknacks and vases, may have memories, but it is dangerous.

## ATTICS, CELLARS AND GARAGES

After a certain point in life, they should be avoided as if they were a combat zone. The probability of accidents in these locales is beyond any simple hints that are anywhere near adequate.

## GENERAL

Furnace, exhaust systems and fireplaces should be checked on an annual basis.

Don't be vain about canes—if they help, use them.

Post emergency numbers in large print by the telephone.

Better yet, get a phone with large numbers that also has a preset dialing system for your emergency numbers.

Consider subscribing to a telephone emergency response system.

Pets can be dangerous—the little ones can trip you and the large friendly ones can knock you over. However, the advantages of pets in the homes of the elderly far outweigh the disadvantages. Obedience school for large unruly dogs is recommended, and care should be taken when going to the kitchen to feed a hungry pet.

Provide a fenced area for dogs to avoid the necessity of walking them in bad weather.

Do not wear high heels. Wear sensible shoes that fit, with nonskid soles.

Purchase a cordless phone to carry in the yard or to remote areas of the house.

Clean all spills immediately. Liquids are an obvious hazard; even talcum powder is a serious fall hazard on an uncarpeted surface.

All door knobs should be replaced with levers or handles.

Purchase irons, toaster ovens or any other heat producing appliances that have an automatic shut-off feature.

## STRETCHING THE BUDGET

At the time of retirement, the average middle-class couple will have Social Security benefits and perhaps a corporate pension or some other form of savings or annuity plan. This monthly income may be adequate but, except for inflation indexing for Social Security, it will be fixed. There will be no future promotions or extra wages for overtime. In other words, the homeowner will need to stretch shelter dollars.We review below several areas that might be investigated by those who need to conserve money in order to remain in their own homes.

### WEATHERIZATION AND INSULATION

In the northern parts of the country, home heating is a major budgetary item. Anticipation of this, prior to retirement, might inspire homeowners to insulate and install thermal windows. These are big-ticket items and hopefully will be installed prior to living on a fixed income.

Often overlooked is the hot water heater. Blanketing this appliance, lowering its temperature setting slightly and attaching use-timer devices can significantly reduce your fuel or electric bill. Many utility companies will perform some of these alterations at little or no charge.

The installation of individual room thermostats, if feasible, will allow heat control for those parts of the house that now receive little or no use. Turning off radiators in those rooms will also produce marked savings.

### HIDDEN INCOME IN THE GARAGE

In densely populated areas, a ready market for garage rentals usually exists. Many retirees may have unused garage space that can be leased to neighbors for their extra car or for storage space.

### ACCESSORY APARTMENTS

Creating an apartment in a single-family dwelling can have several benefits:

1.  It can provide extra income.
2.  A younger tenant might provide chore services as part of the rental agreement.
3.  Other people in the building can create a sense of security that many older owners appreciate.

4.   For those retirees who intend to do a great deal of traveling, a tenant provides a built-in house sitter.

The accessory apartment must be a self-contained unit, which means a full bath and kitchen. In a home with a walk-in cellar this might be done at little cost, but in a home requiring a dormer or other modifications, the costs may make the endeavor economically unfeasible.

Many local zoning laws prohibit accessory apartments. However, some town governments exempt the elderly from these regulations. In these instances, they often either allow the retired homeowner to construct such an apartment or allow the children of the elderly to create an apartment in their home for their parents.

This subject is discussed at greater length in Chapter 8.

## REAL ESTATE TAX BREAKS

Retired homeowners on low fixed incomes should investigate local government regulations concerning deferrals for their property taxes. Many communities have established programs for their older citizens that defer property taxes after they exceed a certain proportion of income. In many instances, these deferred payments are not due until the home is sold or until they become a lien against the estate.

This concept is often underutilized simply because elderly homeowners are not aware that it exists. Phone your local tax assessor to see whether your community has such a program and, if so, what its provisions are.

# ENJOYING YOUR EQUITY
# (HOME EQUITY CONVERSION)

If a homeowner has a small balance on his or her old first mortgage, the bank will be more than pleased to rewrite that ancient 6% loan. As a new borrower, you will receive a very large check that represents up to 80% of your home equity. However, the new mortgage rate is likely to be nearly double the old, and the new payments may make you gasp for breath. Then there is the alternative of the home equity loan, which is actually nothing more than a second mortgage. This debt will run for a shorter period of time than your first mortgage, with a higher rate of interest and payments that also will make you gasp.

These alternatives are not viable for the retired on fixed incomes who hope to control their budgets. But there is another way to benefit from your appreciation besides outright sale of the property, and that is a home equity conversion loan.

This kind of real estate loan is also known as a reverse annuity mortgage, reverse mortgage, sale leaseback or deferred payment loan. All are structured so that either a lump-sum payment or regular monthly payments are made to the *borrower*. The owners remain in the home and the loan is repaid when the house is sold or when the owners die.

A reverse annuity mortgage (RAM) is a low fixed-rate loan that is repaid upon sale of the home or the death of the last surviving owner. A typical RAM on a free and clear $100,000 home will advance up to $80,000, which would be paid out at the rate of $401 a month to the owners for a period of 10 years, or $350 a month for 10 years if a $5,000 lump-sum payment is also taken. All payments would be tax free because they are a loan. If the house is sold at the end of the 10-year period, closing costs and the interest are deducted from the face amount of the loan. If the house is not sold at the end of the 10-year period, the monthly payments would stop, payment would not be required but interest would continue to accumulate.

In Connecticut, for example, the maximum state-sponsored loan amount is $120,000 and the program is restricted to those with family incomes of less than $15,600 in the poorest county, to $26,000 in the wealthiest. There are also private banks that make these loans, in which case the income levels, and in some instances the maximum amount of the loan, do not apply. Interest rates are higher, however.

The federal government has recently become interested in this innovative program, and Congress has approved funding for a demonstration program. The FHA presently has authority to make 2,500 of these loans, of which not more than 50 can be written by any individual lender.

A variation of the RAM plan is the sales plan, in which case the owners actually sell the house, but retain a life estate that allows them to remain for as long as they live, either with or without rental payments. Another variation is the split equity plan, which allows the owners to remain and receive monthly payments; however, their ownership percentage declines proportionately with each payment received.

The variations on and availability of these plans vary not only from state to state but also within states. We suggest that anyone interested in this opportunity contact your local Area Agency on Aging or State Department on Aging. Care must be taken before entering into any of the private programs, and consultation with a reputable real estate attorney is recommended.

The whole concept of reverse mortgages for the elderly is relatively new and has been slowly evolving over the last decade. At present only about 30 states have such programs available, and in some of those states well-meaning legislatures have muddied the waters for RAM. Massachusetts, for example, does not allow variable-rate mortgages for the elderly, and since the secondary mortgage market requires variable-rate mortgages, private lending in RAM is difficult in that state. Missouri has also restricted this type of lending; other state regulations have diluted this program as well.

It seems only just that elderly on strict budgets should be able to enjoy at least some of the real estate appreciation they have accumulated. On the other hand, there is real fear that private lending without oversight would allow unscrupulous operators to literally cheat the elderly out of their homes. A comprehensive federal program within HUD, with uniform state standards, has been suggested.

# YOUR HOUSE, YOUR LIFE

Although there are a host of reasons to sell a house now too large and move to smaller and more convenient accommodations, the pull of memories and habit is strong. The biggest single error committed by those who remain in their homes is the failure to anticipate their future status. A few simple safety precautions may make the difference between a pleasurable old age and a miserable one.

Many communities offer property tax reductions for older residents. The difference is then paid on sale of the home or from the estate. Too few of the elderly avail themselves of these alternatives.

Home equity conversion loans are an interesting new concept that allow owners to benefit from their real estate appreciation, but care should be taken in selecting one of these plans.

# CHAPTER 3

# RETIREMENT COMMUNITIES:
## Retirement Villages or Adult Communities

## WHAT ARE THEY?

Leon A. Pastalan, writing in the Summer 1985 issue of *Generations* magazine, reviewed the results of his group's study of retirement communities and defined them as *"aggregations of housing units with at least a minimal level of services planned for older people who were predominantly healthy and retired."*

Occupancy in a retirement community can be on either a rental or ownership basis. Ownership may assume any one of several forms: orthodox single-family homeownership, co-operative (rare) or condominium (common) ownership. In almost all instances the community provides certain basic services, such as lawn, garbage and recreational facilities, for a monthly fee. Other amenities helpful to the retired, such as transportation vans, may or may not be provided.

For purposes of this discussion, we are excluding retirement housing that provides certain elements of health care as part of the "package" (life-care communities), and other facilities that provide some elements of assisted living (congregate housing). These facilities will be considered later. Retirement communities will be considered for those retirees who are capable of fully independent living and who live in units where some elderly oriented services are provided.

## A GENERATIONAL BATTLE

In March 1989 a federal law took effect that prohibits housing discrimination against families with minor children, after a HUD survey discovered that nearly one-quarter of all new housing in the country specifically excluded small children, while nearly half of all new housing had some provisions that restricted children. Senior citizen housing can be exempt from this statute if 80% of the units have at least one resident over the age of 55 *and* they "provide significant facilities and services specifically designed to meet the physical and social needs of older persons." There is a great deal of discussion as to exactly what constitutes "significant facilities and services." Life-care communities with skilled nursing homes and congregate housing with their assisted living provisions obviously qualify under this exclusion. Retirement communities usually qualify under the age mandates, but they must also provide other services for the elderly. Transportation vans, wheelchair access to all facilities and a recreational program directed toward older individuals would probably be adequate to qualify for exemption.

# WHERE ARE THEY?

Before World War II, retirement communities as we now think of them simply did not exist. There were only small enclaves of retirees in Miami Beach, along with a few trailer parks with many gray heads in southern California.

Today, if we were to mention the premier retirement community, we might think of Del Webb's Sun City, in Arizona, with its population of 47,500 senior citizens. Next in line might be California's Leisure World, with a population of nearly 30,000. These are more than communities, they are new towns that cater to the retired.

Sun City, northwest of Phoenix, has 11 golf courses, eight lawn bowling greens, 72 shuffleboard courts, seven swimming pools, and 17 tennis courts. It has five auditoriums, with many studios and game rooms for hobbies and crafts. Its six shopping centers boast 350 stores, 16 restaurants, 15 branch banks and its own local newspaper. New residents must be over 50 years of age; they are generally under 75 and in good health.

In contrast, we discovered a small retirement community in Florida that consisted of fewer than 30 lots for mobile homes, a very small swimming pool and an open pavilion that passed as the recreation hall.

The Pastalan study, which performed most of its field work in the 1970s and which utilized certain technical exclusions, was able to identify only 2,300 retirement communities. It also stated that they ". . . are most commonly found in Sunbelt and western states with climates conducive to year-round outdoor activity."

Florida officials estimate that more than 2,500 mobile (manufactured) home developments in that state are retirement communities. Prior to 1965 there was virtually no nongovernmental building of these communities in northern states. In that year, Heritage Village of Southbury, Connecticut, began construction of 3,000 retirement condominium units. At the time, this was considered to be a revolutionary marketing gamble, but the success of this project has vindicated the concept.

Because of the kinds of ownership mix, diverse locations and wide range of services, there is no practical method to count the number of these communities that may presently exist or are under construction.

## RETIREMENT COUNTIES

The Federal Department of Agriculture classifies 487 counties in the United States as nonmetropolitan retirement counties, using as its standard of measurement a population increase of 15% that can be attributed to elder migrations.

Sullivan County, in the Catskill Mountains north of New York City, is considered a retirement county, as were Cape May and Ocean Counties in New Jersey until they were recently reclassified as urban counties. Grand County in Oklahoma and Dare County in North Carolina are other examples. Real estate interests in Idaho, Arkansas and Alabama have lobbied their legislatures to promote this concept within those states as well.

The original inhabitants of these counties seem to have mixed feelings toward the new arrivals. They are pleased at the influx of affluent retirees, who pay prime prices for land and do not burden school systems. However, they have also discovered that the new jobs created by these population shifts have been almost exclusively in the low-paid service industries. In fact, some retirement counties have inadvertently discouraged new high-tech industry because of the rise in land prices and the aging of the work force.

Some developers in these rural areas have taken their marketing approach one step further and created retirement communities with a specific appeal. Worman's Mill, near Frederick, Maryland, is modeled after an old farmer's village, for example, and William's Hill, not far from Providence, Rhode Island, is a reproduction of an old New England village. Byron Park, in Walnut, California, has a decidedly English ambiance.

Information regarding these specialized retirement communities can be obtained from the National Association of Senior Living Industries, 184 Duke of Gloucester Street, Annapolis, Maryland 21401.

### THERE'S RETIREMENT IN THEM THAR HILLS

Prentice-Hall publishes a *Retirement Places Rating Guide*, by David Savageau (third edition, 1990); another popular book on the same subject is *Retirement Choices: For the Time of Your Life*, by John Howells (Gateway

Books, 1987). These guides have rating systems based on geographic characteristics, crime rates, housing prices, other costs, climate, recreational activities, health care and other factors of interest to retirees. A study of these books can turn up possibilities that the retiree might easily never discover otherwise.

A comparison of these guides reveals that they often differ in their choices simply because many of the characteristics considered are subjective. Although these books will not be gospel in their selections, they are worth scanning.

If your retirement consideration does include a possible relocation, and you have developed an interest in several distant areas, try subscribing to the local newspaper, daily or weekly. Read the classified and general ads carefully. These small-town newspapers can be very revealing about costs, and you will be able to determine the price of eating out, purchasing general services, real estate values and something about the social environment and problems of the area. The local political issues as revealed in news articles, ads and party statements might reveal potential problems. For example, if there are fights about establishing a toxic dump in the area, the lack of hurricane insurance after the last blow-out, or curing the acid rain problem, you may not wish to live there.

It is not uncommon for remote areas to have a two-tier price structure for real estate. The locals know the "real" price of mountain land may be less than $100 an acre. The "outsiders," through a development company, may be offered identical land at $1,000 an acre. These price disparities work because the retirees may have lived their adult lives in metropolitan areas or high-density suburbs where even at $1,000 an acre the property seems dirt cheap. A careful reading of local real estate offerings might be the first indication that such two-tier pricing is endemic to the area. Similarly, statistical information from the local chamber of commerce or appropriate state agencies may be self-serving, but it can also be revealing. Many isolated rural areas simply do not have enough doctors to serve their present inhabitants, much less an influx of retirees. In past years, the National Health Service assigned many young doctors to these areas, but budgetary cutbacks in this service have vastly curtailed these programs.

Care should be taken to research the availability of skilled nursing homes in an area, the quality of the local hospital and its ability to handle most emergencies. Geriatric assessment centers are found in large medical centers and would not be expected in a retirement county, but ideally there should be one within a day's drive.

## THE NATIVES AREN'T ALWAYS FRIENDLY

It seems paradoxical, but it is nevertheless true, that the original inhabitants of isolated areas often resent newcomers. This not only exists where they are financially dependent on the new arrivals but, in fact, seems to increase proportionately to that dependence. The friction between town and gown or winter versus summer people has always been a fact of life. The original residents of retirement counties were isolated and often impoverished. They often look upon retirees as "privileged."

By nature, if not by definition, retirement counties are somewhat remote and underdeveloped, with cheap land and low construction costs. The fact that they are usually scenic is an added attraction. However, those opting for this retirement alternative should realize that the natives are not going to welcome them into their political and social institutions without difficulty. Retirees in these areas tend to be friends with other newcomers, and in a sense two societies coexist.

## A RETIREMENT COUNTY WARNING

Beware of winterizing without checking out all the facts before you purchase the property. It is not uncommon for individuals to purchase a summer home with the intent of improving, winterizing and eventually utilizing it as a permanent retirement residence in the future. Local regulations or conditions may make this future possibility impractical or impossible.

Many lake and shore areas do not have sewage systems and depend upon archaic septic systems with ground conditions that have extremely low percolation rates and high water tables. While these areas might tolerate short-term summer use, they are not capable of sustaining year-round use without overflow or contamination. As a consequence, the communities may prohibit the issuance of building permits for heating systems, etc., therefore restricting the use of the property.

Lots in isolated wooded areas are often sold with access by private road. These roads, perhaps owned by large paper companies, may not be maintained during the winter. Homes in such situations are accessible as long as the owners are proficient in the use of snowshoes.

# CALL OF THE SUN BELT

## A FLORIDA OVERVIEW

Although Sun Belt retirement communities exist in a number of states, Florida gets one in four of all those retirees who move from their state of origination. Nearly 17.8% of Florida residents are over the age of 65. Of the 20 U.S. cities with the largest concentration of elders, 16 of them are in Florida. Fifteen thousand elderly migrate to this state each month.

Weather is a prime factor. A good portion of the state is below the frost line, with a temperate climate year round. Besides increasing comfort levels, this also means lower heating and construction costs. Conventional homes can be constructed on concrete slabs, while manufactured homes can be set on concrete blocks.

Florida has encouraged this elder migration by its low inheritance taxes, lack of state income tax and its homestead property tax exemption. Under the homestead exemption, the first $25,000 of a primary dwelling's worth is exempt and, in the case of those over 65 years of age, an additional $5,000 is exempt.

Hundreds of retirement communities are scattered throughout Florida. Recently, the high cost of land has driven up prices on the Gulf and ocean, so new developments in those areas tend to be high-rise condominiums. Single-family developments are now constructed primarily in central Florida. Prices can range from a low of $25,000 for a manufactured home on a rental lot to more than $1 million for an estate on waterfront property.

## AN INFORMAL FLORIDA SURVEY

The authors made an informal survey of more than 30 retirement communities in Florida. Almost all of those surveyed were located in central Florida, and all consisted of individual homes. The number of lots involved ran from a low of 43 per project to a high of 1,500. The average development size was 520 units. The price ranged from $15,900 for a manufactured home on a rented lot to $134,700 for a three-bedroom free-standing home.

In the projects surveyed, mobile homes (manufactured homes) outnumbered conventional construction by two to one. All of the conventional builders offered lots as part of the total home price, while the mobile home builders stressed lot rentals, although many had sections within their projects where lots could be purchased.

If lots were purchased, the village fees ran from $25 to $100 a month to cover community maintenance. Each village had at least one recreational building.

Each retirement community included in its monthly fees exercise and craft rooms, garbage pickup, sewer and grounds maintenance, tennis courts and swimming pools. Golf course and marina use was almost always an extra expense. Lot size tended to be a quarter acre, except in the small mobile home communities.

The smallest housing units ran from 600 to 800 square feet of interior living space and usually cost $40,000, including lot, for conventional construction, and $36,500, without lot, for manufactured homes. Lot rentals averaged $235 a month.

The larger homes, more than 2,000 square feet, cost $100,000 or more for conventional construction, or $54,500 for manufactured homes, without lots. The largest manufactured homes were considerably smaller than the largest conventionally constructed homes.

## MARCIA AND AL

Marcia and Al were competitive sports people. They exhibited these qualities in their business and personal lives. Business was a game you played to win, and the prize was economic gain. For relaxation they participated in outdoor sports during the daylight hours and cut-throat bridge at night. They skied during the winter, golfed in the spring and fall and honed their tennis skills during the summer months.

As they grew older, they sensibly replaced downhill skiing with cross-country and cut their golf games down to 18 holes from their usual 36 holes. They replaced tennis with racquetball. At retirement, they knew exactly the type of community they desired and quickly purchased a unit in a Florida retirement community, Gulf Country Club Homes. It promised an active life.

When Al developed congestive heart failure he tempered his golf game by using a cart. In his 72nd year he suffered a massive coronary on the 14th hole after a successful chip shot from a bunker.

Six months later, Marcia married a widower who lived three doors down the street. Her new husband was not a golfer, but did play excellent bridge.

Marcia never regretted moving to Gulf Country Club Homes.

## RUTH AND GEORGE

Ruth and George purchased their retirement home in Gulf Country Club Homes because the golf fees were extra. George happily announced that those who didn't play that silly game, didn't pay for that silly game. In many retirement communities, he pointed out, you paid for the upkeep of the golf course whether you participated or not.

Ruth and George were readers. Their idea of a pleasant evening was a steak and salad for dinner, and then the remainder of the evening with a good book. Their nights out were often a meal at a French restaurant followed by a foreign film.

Before purchasing at Gulf Homes they had neglected to determine that the nearest library was 30 miles away, and foreign films were not shown anywhere in the county. They didn't play bridge or other games, although they did like crossword puzzles. Their exercise usually consisted of a brisk walk, but they soon discovered that these were not practical in the hot sun of a Florida summer.

After eight months, they sold their home at a loss and moved back to their native New England.

## A LESSON TO BE LEARNED

Sun Belt retirement villages not only reflect the personality of their developer, but also what he perceives as his market. Advertising for these communities stresses an independent and active life-style. Marketing for these southern projects assumes that their prospects play golf, fish, swim, square dance and socialize like crazy with like-minded others. There is a close parallel between their approach and that of resort hotels and cruise ships.

If this is the type of retirement you desire, the condition of the golf course may be more important than the layout of the house. However, remember that, even for those so inclined, activities appropriate at 65 may become difficult by 75. Retirement communities tend to cater to and service the younger retirees. Many people, as they age, tend to move back to their original locations or into alternative housing, where medical care is more important than the wait for tee-off time.

For those individuals who in the past took their vacations on remote mountain lakes, Sun Belt retirement communities will have little appeal.

## RELOCATION CONSIDERATIONS

### IF YOU WANT TO WORK

Most American men leave the work force before the age of 63. In large companies, those with more than 1,000 employees, the average age of retirement is under 60. Most women leave the work force under age 60. These people are still young and active, and for economic or other reasons may wish to work, either full or part time. Sun Belt or retirement counties are not the place to live if you desire some type of employment. There just aren't many jobs in those places! If you want to work, the place to live is near a moderate-size or large urban area. Because large retirement communities require great amounts of reasonably priced acreage, they are often located in rather remote areas. This places them outside of normal commuting range to urban areas where work might be more readily available.

### TAKE A TRIP

There are now federal regulations meant to eliminate certain abuses in the interstate sale of land. The days of outrageous advertising claims are now gone. However, some abuses still exist. Retirement communities often sell at a distance. A favorite tactic is the free reception-dinner-presentation at a local motel. A sophisticated slide, video, or film presentation opens the program, followed by a question-and-answer period with the "right" questions coming from shills in the audience. Dinner follows, with a project salesperson situated at each table, whose function is to close deals and obtain a minimum deposit.

Purchasing a pig in a poke is the most charitable way to characterize falling for this approach. Many remote retirement communities offer vacation visits to the project. Airfare rebates, some free meals and extremely reasonable room or cottage charges make these get-away trips appealing. In actuality the visit is one long sales pitch. Time is scheduled so that comparison shopping among competitive projects is impossible. The pressure to "sign" is constant.

Failure to visit and thoroughly investigate a retirement community before purchase or rental is obviously imprudent, but so is relying on the visiting arrangements made by the project's sales office. A visit must be made, but on your terms.

Several travel agencies have recently developed programs to aid in this search. These tours will often cover as many as 10 communities at rates that are the equivalent to similar regional sightseeing tours. These tours range from 8 to 15 days and can be helpful in narrowing your choices.

In these specially designed tours, the control of time rests with the travel agent. Sales representatives are invited to "make their pitch," but certain sales tactics are discouraged. The pressure to sign and make just a small deposit is absent.

The National Tour Association, a trade group, can provide names of the travel agencies that arrange these tours, as can the American Association of Retired Persons travel program department.

# ARE THEY FOR US?

There is no question that Sun Belt retirement villages are for the youngest of those in the elderly housing continuum. They are designed for the agile and active. Local villages are more apt to stress convenience, carefree living and security. Whether they are a personal option is a question of taste and preference.

| Advantages | Disadvantages |
| --- | --- |
| Recreational opportunities | We're not as interested in games as we used to be. |
| Stress on active living | Frantic activity |
| Socialization | Communities are often run by cliques. |
| People your own age | Age segregation is dull. |
| No small children underfoot | Limitations put on how long young visitors can stay. |
| Convenient | Isolated |
| Secure premises | Too far from old neighborhood |

| Advantages | Disadvantages |
|---|---|
| Maintenance free | Too many rules |
| Good housing value | Overbuilding has resulted in poor re-sale value for Belt retirement homes. |
| Good unit design | They all look alike. |
| Manufactured homes are very reasonable. | Mobile homes are glorified house trailers. |
| Interior and exterior space is easy to manage. | The lots are tiny or the units are attached. |

# YOUR OWN BACK YARD

Market research has recently convinced retirement community developers that people do not necessarily want to move to the Sun Belt. In fact, they usually do not even want to leave their own state. Del Webb's latest venture is Sun City Las Vegas, far nearer to the California population centers than the Arizona project. The Cenvil Corporation, developer of Century Village Retirement centers throughout Florida, is now constructing Carillon, a retirement community of 8,100 units in Plainfield, Illinois, only 30 miles from Chicago. Leisure Technology, based in Los Angeles, has recently constructed more than 17,000 elderly housing units in New York, New Jersey and southern California.

The Marriott and Hyatt hotel chains, which are entering the elderly housing market, are not building in the Sun Belt but are involved in projects closer to northern and western urban centers. Recent market research studies seem to indicate that retirement communities draw most of their potential customers from a 20- to 30-mile radius.

## IS THIS WHERE YOU WANT TO LIVE?

Wherever the retirement community is located, there will be many restrictions attached to the sale or lease of the property. There will be age restrictions within the federal guidelines, and a host of other regulations, ranging from the poundage allowed for a pet, to prohibitions against exterior antennas, parking in the street or drive, and for-sale signs, as well as standards for exterior decor.

The authors have a relative who purchased a home in a retirement community and promptly painted his front door red. This individual had spent 30 years of his working life in the Far East, where red doors are a traditional symbol to ward off evil spirits. Our relative was not convinced of their efficacy, but he still found red doors charming. However, community restrictions that said the door did not conform carried the day, and our angry relative sold his house at a loss and moved.

Retirement communities have a definite bias toward certain groups. One video tape in our possession opens with a long shot of a large Catholic church located immediately adjacent to the community. The voice-over extols the virtue of the architecture of this particular church building, and then the camera moves toward the community gates and its elaborate security system.

Retirement communities will often extol the retiree's entry into a new era, a new phase, a new start in life. However, their mailings, personal interviews and other publicity will pointedly indicate where the other new residents came from, the companies they worked for and their job titles. The approach is not sophisticated and the message is clear: "These are people like you." Needless to say, it would be wise to make sure that you really want to live among this particular group.

## CONCLUSION

Retirement communities average from 4,000 to 5,000 residents, although some are as large as 40,000 and many house only a few dozen. At present, their major areas of concentration are in Arizona, California, Florida and New Jersey. The method of ownership can vary, although condominiums are popular. The type of construction depends on the location and can range from conventional home construction to manufactured homes, A-Frames, or precut log cabins.

The initial communities were primarily constructed in the Sun Belt states, but recently there have been strong movements to create these facilities near all major metropolitan areas.

Some dissatisfaction has been expressed at community regimentation and a life-style that palls as residents age. A difference in marketing techniques can be observed between those communities in the Sun Belt and those elsewhere. The southern communities stess activity, while the northern projects are more apt to emphasize physical security and convenience.

The decision to move to a retirement community located within your state probably means that you have opted for a tradeoff. You are willing to give up some elements of freedom (agreeing to community rules and regulations), in return for smaller and more manageable living quarters coupled with chore service and physical security provided by the community. It is a logical step in life's housing continuum.

It has been found that those who make these local relocations may miss the loss of living space, but this is tempered by a certain relief in not having to maintain a larger dwelling. Old neighborhoods, friends and relatives are still near enough for convenient visits.

Those who choose to relocate to the Sun Belt have added the additional considerations of climate, geography and activities to their menu. This choice is often a selection of a complete way of life. Each individual retirement community that is "activity oriented" has a unique flavor. While these activities may have been very enjoyable during vacations in one's vigorous years, they may pall as a daily and repetitive diet. These relocations away from a lifetime's surroundings and habits may be invigorating for those who truly wish this change, but for others this uprooting will not be satisfying and will eventually lead to a return home, with all the economic loss that may entail.

A temporary rental of at least six months is highly recommended whenever possible. For those who plan a distant relocation, this period will allow an individual or couple to savor the quality of the community and to find out how much they may or may not miss their past homes.

A temporary rental also allows for a true sampling of the communities' restrictions. Rules that may seem insignificant in the abstract may become a continuing source of resentment over a period of weeks or months.

# CHAPTER 4

# RETIREMENT COMMUNITY OWNERSHIP

## CONDOMINIUMS

Although nearly 75% of the retired own their own home, these dwellings are usually single-family homes constructed prior to 1970. In today's society, the recently married often purchase a ''starter'' condominium as their first home, while senior citizens are more likely to move into their first condo when they move to a retirement village. For this reason, the retired may lack the background in condominium ownership that their younger counterparts have, and a closer look at this type of ownership is necessary.

Condominiums are one of the most prevalent forms of home ownership for those seniors who choose to move. This concept allows builder flexibility and can be utilized for high-rise apartments as well as row- and townhouses. A popular concept is the townhouse cluster with park-like areas between the unit groups.

Condominium associations provide for the professional management and maintenance of common areas. This form of ownership is attractive to purchasers because it provides federal income tax benefits, pride of ownership, participation in real estate appreciation and the freedom to resell. Resale in retirement villages may have certain age restrictions and prohibitions on minor children.

Condominium ownership can trace its origins back to ancient Rome. The word comes from two Latin roots meaning common ownership or control. The blossoming of condo developments throughout the country during the past three decades obscures the fact that in most states they weren't even legal until the 1960s.

Condominium purchasers own their units. If they have a mortgage, it is a lien against that particular unit. Real estate taxes are levied against the unit by the local taxing authority and are paid by the dwelling's owner. In addition, each member of the condominium owns a percentage interest in the common areas. These areas might include, but are not limited to, hallways, walks, parking areas, recreational facilities and open land. These common areas are administered by a condominium association whose members are elected by the individual unit owners. One particular development may consist of one or more condominium associations, depending on size and a logical division of responsibilities.

In addition to real estate taxes and mortgage payments, if any, on an individual unit, the owners must also pay a monthly fee to the association for the costs of maintaining the common areas. The size of this fee is determined by the association's annual budget and divided among the owners proportionate to the size of the unit. The holder of a larger unit pays more than the owner of a smaller unit.

The monthly condominium fee (often called common charges or assessment), often pays for maintenance staff wages, trash collection, grounds care, common building repair, common area utilities and real estate taxes. From time to time the board of directors may vote special assessments for nonrecurring expenses or unusual or unanticipated costs.

The association, as managed by the elected board of directors, may administer the condominium directly, or it may hire a professional management firm to perform the day-to-day chores.

# COOPERATIVES

At first glance the differences between a co-op and a condominium may seem minimal, but a further look reveals that although the differences are sophisticated, they are significant. A housing cooperative owns and operates a living facility for the benefit of the occupants, who are also shareholders. Membership in the cooperative is obtained by purchasing these shares, in exchange for which an occupancy agreement grants the right to live in a particular designated unit. The shareholders also elect a board of directors, who may manage the project directly or delegate the authority to a professional management firm.

Real estate financing, the mortgage loan and real estate property taxes are not levied against individual units, but are a lien against the whole project. These costs are paid by the shareholders on a monthly basis, usually called the co-op's maintenance fee. Cooperatives, like condominiums, are subject to special assessments to the owners or shareholders to pay for unforeseen or unusual expenses.

Since individual unit ownership is not involved in a co-op, the board of directors can have a great deal of control over who can purchase shares. Most co-op by-laws include a right of first option for the corporation to purchase a seller's shares or to approve the new buyer. These rules often either prohibit or restrict the right of shareholders to rent their units to outsiders. It is important to remember that in general the co-op board has more authority than its condominium counterpart.

Cooperatives are a valid and, in some instances, as we shall see later, a preferable way to hold real estate title. However, residents of New York City have recently observed the down-side of co-op activity. In New York more than 5,000 rental apartment buildings have been converted to co-op ownership since 1976. Thousands of units in these buildings are still owned by the original sponsors because rent regulation laws allow the original tenants to remain as renters if they elect not to buy their apartment. These regulated rents were often less than the monthly maintenance charges for those units, but while real estate values rose and before the Tax Reform Act of 1986, sponsors utilized tax deductions and the healthy profits made on these units when they finally came on the market to offset their losses. However, with the tax law changes and a soft real estate market, many of these sponsors found themselves in jeopardy.

Lawyers now advise clients contemplating a co-op purchase to request a copy of the co-op's financial statement from the building's management agent. If the sponsor still owns one-third or more of the units, proceed with extreme caution.

Cooperative ownership for retirement housing is virtually unknown in the Sun Belt. Co-ops are usually found in urban areas, most extensively in New York City, where high-rise apartments are the rule. A few nonprofit housing corporations or local housing authorities have started limited-equity cooperatives as a means of providing low-cost senior housing. In a limited-equity cooperative, the member cannot sell his or her shares in the corporation for more than he or she originally paid, plus an agreed upon capped increase. The theory behind this concept is to keep the unit shares affordable for people of moderate income. The federal government does have some cooperative programs such as a section of the HUD Section 8 program, which provides subsidized rent to those who live in tenant-initiated cooperative conversions. At present, the funding for these programs is practically nonexistent so that they are not an important factor in the senior housing market. Two distinct advantages to cooperatives over condominiums is that government subsidy programs usually run to co-ops over condominiums, and property taxes are usually lower since the assessment on a total co-op is less than a number of assessments against individual condominium units.

# MOBILE (MANUFACTURED) HOMES

The only time these manufactured homes are truly mobile is when they move down the highway to the lot. These dwellings are constructed completely in a factory, often to the point where all fixtures, appliances and furnishings are included. These are the "wide load" half houses you see moving slowly down the highways toward their final destinations.

Nearly 200 manufacturers construct these buildings, and, since 1976, they have been subject to construction, durability and safety requirements by the Federal Department of Housing and Urban Development. Manufactured homes now represent nearly one-third of all the new homes sold in this country. They can be as large as three bedrooms with two baths.

In the Florida retirement communities surveyed that sold manufactured homes, financing was offered on an installment contract basis. They usually required 15% down, and interest rates for a 20-year term were competitive with real estate mortgages. The lots were rented from the developer for about $235 a month.

Lot rentals include the land rent, maintenance of common grounds, sewer and water, garbage pick-up, cable TV, planned activities, swimming pools and use of the club house and shuffleboard. Golf and boating were usually not included.

Although most leases claim to be "guaranteed for a lifetime," they are written on an annual basis, with fixed increases of not more than 5% a year or the Consumer's Price Index rate of inflation, whichever is higher.

Manufactured home communities discourage lot purchase, if it is available at all. One developer offers a mobile home for $64,000 without lot, and asks $30,900 for the lot alone plus a $94 a month community fee. The same developer offers the same home without lot for a $200-a-month rental fee, which includes land rent and community fee.

The distinct advantage of a manufactured home on a rental lot is price. An attractive new mobile home in a pleasant Florida community can be purchased for $40,000 with a down payment of $6,000 and reasonable monthly carrying charges.

The primary disadvantage of buying a mobile home on a rental lot is the poor resale value and lack of appreciation. Many experts estimate that a manufactured home on a rental lot depreciates at 10% for the first year of occupancy and 5% for every year thereafter.

Remember, these units are *not* financed by conventional real estate mortgages, but on installment contracts. As the unit ages, the availability of this financing decreases. It is very possible that the owner of such a unit might have to take back the financing in the event of resale, as no institution would be willing to make a loan.

In addition, many legal questions concerning the base land remain unresolved, with the validity of leases and their renewals in question if the original developer either sells or goes under.

In some instances, the mobile home park has been structured as a cooperative. In this instance, the unit owner not only owns his or her home, but also a share in the nonprofit corporation that owns and runs the park.

## OWNING OR RENTING YOUR LOT

The marketing efforts of many Sun Belt retirement communities stress low cost for rented lots and also the developer's continued interest in the project. This practice is so prevalent as to require a further look.

To use a hypothetical example: a $10,000 lot financed by a mortgage at 12% interest for a 15-year term would cost $120 per month, or $21,600 for the term. If the same lot were initially rented at $150 a month and the yearly increases were minimal (usually 5% a year), the 15th year monthly charge would be $220 a month, with total payments for the period of $33,300.

By purchasing the lot, the owner would have saved $11,700 over the 15-year period, the payments would have remained constant at $120 a month, and the lot would belong to the resident at the expiration of the mortgage. In addition, mortgage interest would have been tax deductible. In Florida and some other states a homestead exemption could have reduced property taxes, conventional real estate financing could have been arranged on the complete home rather than an installment contract, and the lot might have appreciated in value. A purchase that includes the lot and allows a true real estate mortgage would extend the term of the loan. This extension would reduce monthly payments, probably by enough to include the purchase of the lot. This fixed-term loan would also mean that future costs are known and can be properly anticipated. It is true that community fees would have been charged in addition, but it is doubtful that the total costs would have exceeded the total rental fees.

As a further breakdown of these costs:

| Monthly cost of lot in 10th year, if owned: | Monthly lot rental in 10th year: |
|---|---|
| $120 mortgage | |
| $ 80 monthly maint. fee | |
| $200 a month | $200 month |

Real estate property tax with a homestead exemption should be about equal to the mobile home license fee and the yearly personal property tax fee.

Until the 10th year it is cheaper to rent the lot; after that time the balance tips toward purchase. Potential resale value is always higher with lot purchase.

In addition, if a developer of a rental project defaults on his loan and the bank forecloses, all leases would be nullified and could be rewritten at a higher amount. Similarly, if the owner dies or sells the property, the new owner might rewrite the lease to the lot renter's disadvantage.

From a consumer's standpoint, lot rentals are a poor investment; in fact, they are not an investment at all. Land rentals make sound economic sense only for those individuals who wish temporary residence in a Sun Belt community with the minimum cash expenditure.

# OTHER FORMS OF CONSTRUCTION

The basic rationale for retirement housing is efficiency of size and cost. These criteria have implied heavy use of mobile, modular and precut construction techniques. These terms should be explained:

**House trailers** have permanently mounted wheels and are pulled by another vehicle. These units can be used for vacation traveling, although some of the larger ones are most often moved directly from the factory to the trailer park, where they are placed on a cement block foundation. They differ from RV vehicles, which have many housing amenities, but which are self-propelled. RVs are very popular with retired couples, who use them for extensive travel. If you own an RV, you should determine if it can be parked on a unit lot before selecting a retirement community. Many villages prohibit parking these vehicles.

Legions of the recently retired opt for a temporary life on the road. Driving RVs or house trailers, these intrepid travelers travel cross-country, often following the seasons and staying in state or national parks, commercial campgrounds or trailer parks. This is an adventuresome mode of life and has its parallel with those who opt for extensive foreign or shipboard travel. It is a way of life that is temporary, and, after some months or years of this activity, these people generally return to their original homes or other forms of alternative housing.

House trailers have a distinct advantage over RVs for those involved in extensive travel. Once parked, the pulling vehicle can be separated for side trips or ordinary use. Those stuck with maneuvering an RV on a day-to-day basis soon wish for this advantage.

As permanent alternative housing, house trailers have three distinct disadvantages: They are not elderly friendly, they can be dangerous and in many northern areas of the country trailer parks are not the most desirable locations. Ordinary house trailers, while adequate for the young or active elderly, have narrow passageways, complicated storage and are generally not practical for those with chronic health problems or difficulty in walking or with other activities of daily living.

House trailers are susceptible to fire and storm. During hurricane or tornado alerts, these are the occupants who are first asked to leave their domiciles for safer quarters.

There are many southern trailer parks built around lakes with recreational amenities as sophisticated as any retirement village. However, in the North these parks tend to have the vehicles parked shoulder to shoulder with few amenities except for a laundry room.

**Modular Housing** consists of fully outfitted components that are built in a factory and then trucked to the site where they are fixed to a standard foundation. One modular unit is not necessarily half a house, but may be any section of the home, or even part of an apartment or condominium complex.

**Precut Homes** are also factory constructed, but are shipped in pieces to the site, where they are reassembled. Log cabin precuts and A-frames are examples of this type of construction.

In the past, local building codes and union requirements restricted the use of many factory-built homes. Recently, with union permission where necessary and with stricter production codes, there has been a greater acceptance of these techniques. Builders like to use them because they decrease construction time, labor costs and reliance on the weather.

# CHAPTER 5

# RETIREMENT COMMUNITY SAFETY HINTS: With Checklist

## YOU LIKE THE PLACE

You have found a retirement community that you like. The price is within your budget. It's located where you want to live. You have compared the price with that of competing projects (remember that extra amenities may add from 5 to 10% to the total cost for senior projects).

Construction standards and unit design features meet your requirements, and a competent engineer has inspected the property. There are other areas, some of which are specific to senior housing, that should be carefully investigated:

## EVEN THE BIGGEST CAN FALL

In April of 1990 General Development Corporation, one of Florida's largest builders, filed for bankruptcy. This action followed its guilty plea to fraudulent sales practices.

Beginning in 1955, this builder constructed nine communities containing more than 38,000 homes. Port St. Lucie and Port Charlotte were two of their well-known projects.

The company's aggressive national sales organization sponsored orientation programs throughout the country and extended invitations for tours of the Florida communities. Its usual method of operation was a vacant lot sale to a prospect, paid for over a 10-year period, during which the developer retained the deed. When a lot owner reached retirement and wished to have a house constructed, the paid-for lot was then used as a down payment. If the purchaser failed to make a payment, the lot reverted to the developer without a foreclosure proceeding.

The crime was that the appraisals given to visitors were 40% higher for homes and often 10 times higher for lots than prevailing local prices. Purchasers often did not discover their problem, since most defaulted on their payouts before the 10-year period expired. If the lot was paid for, only an attempt to finance or resell revealed the inflated appraisals.

The success of General Development's chicanery for so many years is a prime example of the convincing power of marketing glitz. Expensive sales brochures, attractive and articulate sales personnel and guided tours that were whirlwinds of programmed propaganda and activities do convinced many. This approach is not confined to Sun Belt communities, but exists wherever unscrupulous developers have property and prospects have money. This is not to say that most developers are operating illegally, for this is not the case, but they certainly do present their projects in the most favorable light.

The authors asked one sales representative of a Sun Belt community what would happen to a lot lease if the developer went belly up. "That's impossible," the salesperson replied. "The corporation is mostly owned by X, who has millions."

General Development had assets of $863 million and liabilities of $834 million plus a lot of lawsuits when it declared bankruptcy. It is doubtful that this sad state of affairs was revealed to sales prospects.

Whether you are buying, leasing or renting in a retirement community, remember that the sales personnel are on commission. Any representation they make has no validity unless it is backed up by legal documentation from the corporation itself.

Fancy brochures and slide or videotape presentations are also ubiquitous. This marketing material, plus showpiece items such as pools or clubs, are the major startup costs for these projects. Their luxury or tastefulness, unfortunately, give little indication of the projects' true worth.

# YOUR LAWYER

There is a present tendency for law firms to prepare "user-friendly" documents. This means that those long condominium declarations appear to be almost comprehensible to the layperson. Don't let them fool you. We must constantly stress the importance of proper representation at all stages of your real estate activity.

Selecting an attorney from the yellow pages is not adequate, as certain criteria must be considered:

**Local representation.** There are wide differences in the law between the states. Therefore, your kindly Uncle Ned may have represented you in legal matters in New York for a generation, but if you are buying in Florida, you need a local attorney. You must have representation by a member of the state bar in which the property is located.

**Find a lawyer with real estate expertise.** Today lawyers tend to specialize in their practice. It is imperative to locate an attorney with an extensive real estate background.

**At arm's length.** The lawyer who represents the bank making a real estate mortgage on your purchase has interests similar to yours, but they are not identical. The lawyer who represents the builder or developer has interests that are in direct conflict with yours. Your legal representation must be separate from all other interested parties in the transaction.

**Use your lawyer.** Probably the biggest error made by real estate purchasers is *when* they retain a legal representative. After the contract signing is too late! A real estate closing is basically a clerical function, and in many states with escrow offices, it is treated as such. The time when legal advice is most needed is at contract signing. The purchase contract (binder, sales agreements, bond for deed, or whatever its local nomenclature) is the most vulnerable time for the purchaser. Seek local, independent legal advice from a knowledgeable real estate attorney before signing any document!

## How to Find a Good Local Lawyer

A call to the local county bar association will provide a list of several lawyers interested in real estate. All this means is that these are young lawyers who have expressed an interest in real estate and have placed their names on the revolving list for just this type of call.

Almost all public libraries have an annual reference work called the *Martindale-Hubble Law Directory*. This multivolume work lists every lawyer in this country and Canada alphabetically by state and town. There is also a biographical section that indicates their fields of interest and typical clients. If they indicate real estate in their practice, and several builder or banking clients, they are a potential firm for you to contact.

If the retirement community is a large fish in a small pond, and the nearest community lists only a few law firms, we suggest contact be made with a firm in a surrounding town. It is always possible that a large project located in a sleepy hamlet will so dominate the economy as to preclude new purchasers from proper local representation.

# Realtors, Appraisers and Title Insurance

## Realtors

Real estate agents are attractive, pleasant people, and it is often difficult to remember that they do not represent you, the purchaser. The real estate broker or salesperson in any transaction is paid by the seller or developer, not by the borrower or purchaser. A thought to always be kept in mind.

## APPRAISERS

Commercial real estate operates under slightly different standards and has professional categories for appraisers. In a single-family residence, condo, empty lot or whatever, the appraisers are most apt to be local real estate brokers. It is unfortunate, and not always openly dishonest, but these individuals often wish the property were selling at the value they claim for it.

It seems simplistic to say, but value is established only by what other people are willing to pay. In the example of real property, this can be approximated by what they paid yesterday for similar property.

## TITLE INSURANCE

Although nearly all mortgage lenders will require a mortgage title insurance policy to guarantee their loan is a valid first lien, many home buyers do not purchase an owner's title insurance policy. Even reputable attorneys will often state, ''You don't need it as long as the bank's protected.'' In the case of seniors, who may tend to make large cash payments on their retirement homes, an owner's title insurance policy is a must.

# RESALE PROBLEMS

## IT MAY NOT BE YOUR LAST MOVE

Before you make the decision to change residence, you must determine how much you can spend for housing and still retain adequate income for other expenses. Once that figure has been decided, you must factor in the probability that this may not be your final move. If you elect an active lifestyle today, you may need to make a later change, as the natural restraints of aging prove limiting. For those who remain in this housing for several years, either the loss of a spouse or increasing frailty may require relocation. In these instances, the seniors will often opt for assisted living (congregate housing) or a life-care community (see Chapter 10). Whatever the choice, the expense of future closing fees, moving costs and the resale value are important considerations.

## RETIREMENT COMMUNITY RESALE PROBLEMS

In order to build enough units with competitive amenities, these projects are generally built out of commutation range, on vast acreage in semirural counties. In addition to this isolation, they have a certain built-in turnover rate because of occupant deaths and transfers to medical facilities.

In addition, this housing is restricted to sale to seniors, which also reduces its marketability.

Many retirement communities are constructed in phases because of their size. A purchaser in Phase I will probably have difficulty selling a unit five years hence if Phase IV is then under construction. The large appreciation rates real estate has recently enjoyed have come to an end, at least for the foreseeable future. Phased construction projects may have new units selling for at or near the price of a unit purchased several years ago. This does not place the older unit in a competitive situation unless the resale price is dropped considerably.

Many communities carry restrictions prohibiting for-sale signs on the lot. Others require sales to be made through the developer—and it is unlikely that any sales force will push for a resale on a unit in Phase I when Phase IV still has new units available.

It is also unlikely that real estate will appreciate in the foreseeable future as much as it did in the early and mid-1980s. This is particularly true in certain parts of the country where there is a glut in the condominium market. However, certain villages, because of their attractive qualities, will always have above-market appreciation and good resale value. It is therefore important for you to know the local real estate market and the reputation of the builder, or to contact a broker who does.

## WARNING TO SNOWBIRDS

Northern residents who are financially able will often purchase a Sun Belt retirement unit for winter occupancy. This is a pleasant alternative, but has three significant financial pitfalls:

1.  Beware of the developer who sells you a package with cost figures that include rental income. Not only are many areas in the Sun Belt over-built, but renting units anywhere in the off season is problematic at best. The only prudent approach is to base your financial estimates on the assumption that you will earn no rental income. If any is forthcoming, consider it a bonus.
2.  Snowbirds must consider that sometime in the future they may not wish to make that semi-annual trip. If real estate appreciation and resale are not important in your financial picture, fine, but if they are, then it is time to reconsider this alternative. Another Snowbird possibility is to do it on the cheap. Certain Sun Belt communities provide very inexpensive manufactured homes on rental lots with low down payments. Five to 10 years of use, even with poor resale potential, might be an acceptable loss to some.

3. Avoid time-sharing arrangements like the plague. These accommodations are overpriced, are a less than poor investment and have virtually no resale value.

In a typical situation, a $200,000 resort condominium will sell time-share intervals for $10,000 per week. This is a good deal . . . for the developer. Since condominium construction is presently overbuilt in most resort areas and there is no viable secondary market for resale of these time-share intervals, they are not a good investment.

Clinton Burr, a Chicago-based lawyer, formed Resort Property Owners Association in 1988. This organization is a consumer protection group representing 22,000 time-share owners. A survey by Mr. Burr's organization, published in *The New York Times* on June 10, 1990, states that of the 1.5 million time-shares in the country, nearly 500,000 are presently for sale. Nearly one-quarter of these intervals, 340,000, are in Florida, and more than 100,000 of these are presently for sale.

The one-third of the time-share owners presently trying to sell typically paid $10,000 per week, but would sell at any price. Mr. Burr further stated that in the 15-year history of time-sharing only 2.9% of those who have tried to sell have been able to do so, and these usually sold for 50% of the original sales price.

# RETIREMENT COMMUNITY CHECKLIST

## THE COMMUNITY LOCATION

Does it have reasonable access to an interstate highway?

Is it reasonably near mass transportation (including airports)?

Is medical treatment available?

hospital emergency room

doctors' and dentists' offices

ambulance service with trained EMTs

a geriatric assessment center within a day's drive

ancillary medical services such as labs and podiatrists

reliable home health care agencies close enough to properly service the community?

Is there nearby shopping with a variety of different outlets?

## THE EXTERIOR OF THE COMMUNITY

Is there proper physical security—fire and police?

Are the streets and walks well constructed?

Are utility services in?

Is the project at least 80% occupied two years after completion?

Is the exterior maintenance adequate?

Are the common buildings well maintained?

## THE AMENITIES

Are the promised recreational buildings completed?

Are they adequate to serve the proposed community?

Do you like what they offer?

Does the community provide a transportation van with scheduled runs to health offices and shopping centers?

Will the community maintenance staff perform minor chores for the unit owners (plumbing, window washing, etc.)?

## RESTRICTIONS (DEED, COMMUNITY OR ASSOCIATION)

Does your pet satisfy the animal restrictions?

Do parking rules preclude boats, RVs and other special vehicles?

Are the restrictions too confining for your life-style?

Do the restrictions on guests affect your plans?

Are there resale restrictions, such as against for-sale signs?

## THE LIVING UNIT

Is it elder-friendly?

doors wide enough for a wheelchair

well lit without dark corners

kitchen oven at waist level

grab bars in the bath

Is it easily maintained?

## MAINTENANCE FEES (OTHER THAN CONDO OR CO-OP FEES)

Exactly what is included—trash, water, cable?

What is not included?

Is there a cap on how much these fees can be raised?

What is the past history of fee increases?

## OWNERS' ASSOCIATIONS (OTHER THAN CONDO OR CO-OP)

Does one exist?

How are members elected?

What power do they have?

What is their past history in dealing with management?

## THE OTHER RESIDENTS

Are they friendly and open?

Have you spoken to several concerning their experiences in the community?

Would they move here if they had it to do again?

## WARNING FLAGS

Do the salespeople use high-pressure tactics?

Do they sell unimproved building lots years ahead? (This does not include your purchase of raw land for future use, but anticipates small, vacant subdivision lots.)

Do they promise impressive future amenities?

Do they provide all the documentation you request?

Beware of lot rentals, but if required, ask the following—

Is there a cap on the annual rent increase?

Is the lease, by its terms, guaranteed renewable?

What happens in the event of the developer's foreclosure on the land?

What provisions exist for continuation of the lease in the event of renter's death or resale of the home?

## CONDOMINIUM WARNINGS

Beware of time sharing, both personally and in nearby units.

Exceptionally low monthly maintenance payments can be a warning of trouble.

Beware of an excessive number of rentals—they indicate a condo in difficulty.

Beware of a high vacancy rate for the same reason.

What is the unit owner delinquency rate? Some owners may withhold payments to protest poor upkeep.

Have all documents and financial arrangements reviewed by a knowledgeable attorney and accountant.

# CHAPTER 6

# OTHER OPTIONS: Federal- and State-Sponsored Elderly Housing and SROs

## FEDERAL HOUSING PROGRAMS

### HUD

The Department of Housing and Urban Development (HUD) has been tainted by political favoritism, raped by independent escrow agents who misappropriated funds and has even lost millions a year on its single-family home mortgage guarantee program, which was designed to be self-financing. Although in the 30 years of its existence, HUD's Section 202 Program for Elderly and Handicapped housing has had one project foreclosure out of the 200,000 units constructed, the program is apparently being phased out of existence.

In 1979 the program financed 20,000 units. The 1990 funding dropped to 8,368 units, and for 1991 the budget calls for a total of 3,097 elderly units. There is virtually no vacancy rate in the existing apartments. An independent study by the University of Illinois found that an average of eight people were on the waiting list for every vacancy, and this rises to 28 people waiting for newer buildings in metropolitan areas. It is estimated that at present, 250,000 elderly are on project waiting lists.

### HOW 202 WORKS

The 202 program for Elderly and Handicapped rental housing constitutes a low-rate 40-year term direct loan to a nonprofit sponsor. The program is linked to the federal Section 8 rent supplement entitlement for those with low incomes.

The sponsors for these projects must be nonprofit corporations, and typically are religious organizations, minority groups, fraternal orders, labor unions, teacher associations, senior citizen groups and consumer cooperatives.

The HUD *Handbook* for processing these loans states, "Housing the elderly or handicapped requires that special consideration be given to such factors as location and site, architectural and special design features, and the inclusion of a wide range of services and programs . . . sites are selected to avoid steep inclines, noxious odors and the like. Architectural barriers such as steps and narrow doorways are eliminated to assure ingress and egress . . . nonslip flooring, grab-bars . . . health and medical facilities available in the community . . . a variety of recreational activities should be available and encouraged."

The project loan does not include payment for these extra services, and the program does not anticipate assisted living, but assumes that tenants are able to live independently. Meals and other services are not included except under the small pilot Congregate HUD program discussed in Chapter 9.

Because 202 projects are tied to the Section 8 rental assistance program, tenants pay only 30% of their income in rent. At one time becoming eligible for Section 8 rental assistance meant that an individual's income could not exceed 80% of the median income for the community. Recent changes have reduced this criterion to 50% of the median income, and this change has successfully barred the elderly of even modest income from these projects.

## OTHER FEDERAL PROGRAMS

Countless thousands of the retired live in housing either guaranteed or subsidized by HUD, although these units are not specifically designed for the elderly. The chances for the newly retired to move into newer units become increasingly remote as HUD budgets are cut. Appropriations for subsidized housing programs were cut by 75% during the Reagan administration, from $33 billion in 1981 to less than $8 billion in 1988. Simultaneous with these massive budget cuts were increases in construction and land costs, which reduced the completion of new units even further.

Subsidized low-cost housing in general has long waiting lists, of from three to five years, and preference is given to the homeless or displaced. In addition, most of these projects are in the inner cities, which are not the first-choice residence for most elderly. Suburban communities have fought pugnaciously to exclude low-cost housing projects because of the danger they perceive to property values.

Public housing was initially conceived as a way to provide housing at reasonable cost for the working poor, the dependent and the elderly poor. In recent years it has become the housing of last resort for the poorest of the poor. Public housing has become anathema for anyone forced to live there. Its high crime rate and poor appearance has driven away all who could possibly afford to move. The original conception for its creation has been lost.

The Housing Voucher program, for which many elderly qualify, pays a monthly subsidy of the difference between "fair-market" rent and one-third of the tenants' incomes. However, in most metropolitan areas, the true market value is far above any federal consideration. This greatly limits the value of this program, which also does not increase the number of housing units.

The Farmer's Home Administration of the U.S. Department of Agriculture handles projects similar to HUD's in rural areas. Studies have shown that homes owned by the elderly in rural areas are often in marked disrepair. The FMHA housing repair grant was meant to rectify this situation for low-income elderly in rural areas. However, the federal budget for 1991 provided only $10 million for this program.

## PROBLEMS WITH THE FEDERAL PROGRAMS

The once viable 202 program has not only been starved by budgetary restrictions, but the pipeline for allocated projects has been clogged by administrative delays.

Present occupants of 202 projects are aging in place. These units are not equipped, funded or constructed with assisted-living concepts in mind. As men and women age and lose some function, they are often unable to continue to live in these units because essential services are not available. This often results in a nursing home admission, which under different conditions might not have been necessary.

Many of the early 202 projects were architecturally sophisticated in their concepts, attractive and contained common areas for recreation and other uses. Recent HUD rulings have reduced not only the number of units, but also the quality of newer projects. Common areas for libraries, recreation rooms or health services are restricted to 5% of the total area. Two-bedroom units are not allowed, and one-bedroom or efficiency units are restricted to 540 and 415 square feet, respectively. Sprinkler systems are a basic requirement for any type of senior housing, but if local regulations do not require a sprinkler system, HUD will not allow its installation.

## STATE AND LOCAL EFFORTS

State housing finance agencies (HFAs) have struggled valiantly to fill the void left by federal budget cuts. These agencies, found in all states but Arizona and Kansas, have utilized tax-exempt bond issues and tax incentives to aid senior housing. Unfortunately, the Tax Reform Act of 1986 eliminated many of the possible tax incentives, and high interest rates on bonds raise the cost of development money. This combination has translated into high rents that, in most instances, price the elderly out of rent supplement payments and discourage sponsors.

On a local level, many communities have offered builders property-tax abatements to include a certain number of low-cost senior housing units in their projects. This was a painless way to provide housing without expending tax dollars. Unfortunately, these inducement programs have foundered with the recent tightening of the real estate market.

## THE FUTURE

Federal and state budgetary problems are the primary reason for the recent limiting of low-cost elderly housing. It is doubtful that there will be a significant improvement in the near future. Caught in this fiscal squeeze will be the elderly of moderate income who are not home owners.

# SROS

Single-room-occupancy units consist of a single room in an apartment building, rooming house, residential hotel or a permanent unit in a transient hotel or motel. Ten-year-old studies indicate that in the 1970s 80,000 to 397,000 people over 65 lived in these quarters.

Until the 1990 census data is assimilated, there is insufficient information to assess the number of elderly presently living in SROs. It is expected, however, that the number has dropped significantly. The movement of welfare families into remaining SROs has driven many elderly from these quarters. Moreover, the destruction and conversion of SRO buildings have also removed many rooms from this use. Although only a portion were occupied by the elderly, it is estimated that more than one million SROs have been torn down since the 1970s, when cities began to rejuvenate their downtown areas.

Under a small "Shelter Plus Plan," HUD in 1991 will fund 1,305 SRO rooms in housing projects and/or rooming houses.

A strict definition of SRO excludes any unit with cooking facilities, although the hidden hotplate and food on the fire escape are common. This narrow definition bypasses countless thousands of rooms and suites once occupied by the elderly in residential hotels of past grandeur. These tiny apartments were advertised as having "efficiency kitchens" which, more often than not, consisted of a hot plate and minuscule refrigerator stuffed into a closet-like space.

Every city possessed these fading residential hotels, which were several steps above the skid-row flop houses. Fifty years ago, prior to decent motel construction, they housed traveling businessmen, actors on tour and permanent residents of advancing age. Their elegance began to fade, but, prior to gentrification of the area, they still housed countless elderly of moderate income. The many hotels on Manhattan's Upper West Side are a good example of the typical cycle these buildings have experienced. At the turn of the century they housed, on a semipermanent basis, people such as Enrico Caruso. After the 1920s they became almost exclusively a permanent home for the elderly. After several decades of this use they were utilized by New York City to house welfare families. Gentrification of the area in the 1970s and 1980s made it economically attractive to convert the structures to condominiums, which were sold primarily to the younger affluent.

This same pattern of change from affluence to fading gentility to poor to affluence again has been repeated over and over again in every major city. Consequently, the SRO is not a viable alternative for the elderly in most areas of the country. Where such units still exist, they are few in number and temporary at best.

# WHAT NEXT

The occupants of single rooms in hotel-like settings were often isolated individuals. Sociological studies often identified them as "loner types." These living accommodations offered nothing in the way of services for seniors; they merely provided space to house those on limited income.

It is unfortunate that HUD's 202 Program for elderly housing has been the victim of budgetary restraints. Since many of these projects were located in urban areas, they often housed the very people dislocated by the disappearance of the SROs.

At the present time our senior citizens and their advocacy groups have been very active politically in protecting their interests under Medicare and Social Security legislation. It is hoped that as more permanent answers are reached in these areas, that more direction and energy will be focused on senior housing, and the HUD and state programs. Everyone in this age bracket should certainly inform their congressional representatives and senior organizations of their continuing interest in these matters.

# CHAPTER 7

# REMAINING INDEPENDENT: What Help Is Available in the Community?

## GOING AGAINST THE ODDS

It is nearly a cliché that independence does not come without struggle. This is certainly true in the case of those elderly faced with declining physical abilities and the onset of chronic disabilities. An active lifestyle at 69 is not difficult. However, the independent 80-year-old must anticipate potential problems and possibly obtain at least some outside assistance.

The loss of privacy and of the ability to make many small daily decisions that any form of congregate (assisted living) entails may not be palatable to the fiercely independent. Even these rugged individuals must be aware that if they live alone, as their mobility decreases they may be faced with problems of socialization, nutrition and perhaps even mental equilibrium. Studies of the elderly have shown that social isolation can cause depression, substance abuse, lack of proper eating habits and poor health monitoring. Social contact alone might help overcome these grim alternatives.

Married couples are often faced with the problem of unequal aging. One partner might be alert, mobile, and free of debilitating ailments. The other might be mentally confused or experiencing chronic illness that requires some degree of nursing care or other assistance.

If one elderly person is to be the primary caregiver to another, a careful assessment of his or her abilities must be done to see whether the caregiver is physically and emotionally able to perform the necessary functions. Time and again, social workers and geriatric case managers report vivid instances of the frail elderly caring for the frail. If outside help is required, needs must be carefully matched against the services that are available.

Social isolation, care for a spouse or simply a heavy household chore that is now difficult or dangerous are problems that must be overcome in order

64

for the elderly to maintain their independence. Unfortunately, there are few comprehensive programs that address this mix of needs, but there are often individual answers.

## FINDING OUT WHAT'S THERE

In some parts of the country the necessary senior services simply do not exist. In other areas they are so fragmented as to become difficult to locate and utilize. The tragedy of many nursing home admissions is that minimal outside assistance might have allowed those individuals to remain in their own homes.

There are a confusing array of services for the elderly that are often hidden within the community. Without proper direction, it can sometimes be difficult to find the proper organization, or to realize that a given service is available at low or moderate cost. Even with the knowledge that a given service does exist, it might still be difficult to locate because of name confusion or because it operates under the umbrella of another organization.

An amendment to the Older Americans Act attempted to rectify this problem by establishing Area Agencies on Aging. An important part of their function is information and referral. There are 700 of these organizations located in every state of the Union. They too can be difficult to find since they may be located within another regional agency under another designation. Once found, they will have a great deal of information regarding the availability of services. If you cannot locate your local Area Agency, contact your state Department of Aging for the proper referral.

Members of the clergy are another excellent source of elderly service information. Large blocks of aging parishioners and the creation of church senior social programs have involved many of the clergy in elder affairs. In order to serve these needs, many clergy have investigated the availability of community services.

The Visiting Nurse Associations spend a great deal of their time in home nursing care for the elderly. These duties have required them to learn what is available in their communities.

Doctors in family practice, nursing home social workers or hospital discharge planners must of necessity be alert to what services are available. A local senior center large enough to have a professional staff will have individuals knowledgeable about service availability.

## WHAT'S NEEDED

There is an immense breadth in the scope of services needed to allow most elderly to remain independent in their own homes. These services can range from extensive skilled nursing care to occasional chore aid with lawns or heavy housework. Some elderly will require neither of these but will occasionally drop into the local senior center for a social afternoon. The key to independence may rest in the availability of transportation vans for those who can't drive or a few hours of respite care for the harried wife caring for a difficult Alzheimer's patient.

## ONE STATE AND ONE CITY'S ANSWER

At a cost of $35 million, Wisconsin provides a Community Option Program for 3,700 elderly and 3,000 handicapped. The state will obtain *any* necessary service to keep an individual from becoming a nursing home resident, as long as the total monthly cost is less than nursing home charges. Cost to the recipient is either free or based on a sliding income scale.

Wisconsin will provide home nursing care, chore service and even arrange for a neighbor to milk the cows, if that is what it takes to continue to maintain a person in his or her own home.

The Senior Home Care Organization in Boston, Massachusetts, helps some 3,000 elderly to remain in their own homes and apartments. Utilizing a vast network of volunteers, this group aids the elderly with house cleaning, dressing, meals, chores and transportation.

# COMMUNITY SERVICES

## SENIOR CENTERS

Senior Centers have evolved over the years from simply places for social gatherings of those over 65, to, in some cases, sophisticated organizations providing a host of services to hundreds of individuals. There is hardly a community of any size that does not offer some sort of senior center. The smaller groups may meet in a church basement or the school cafeteria, while the larger centers may have their own building with a paid, trained staff. It is common for housing projects to sponsor a center, while others are formed by public or volunteer agencies.

The programs can range from social gatherings several afternoons a week to daily lunches at moderate cost, health assessments, senior counseling, transportation vans and a full information and referral service. Because of their diversity, it is difficult to calculate their exact number, but it is estimated that between 11,000 and 12,000 centers exist throughout the country. Their initial funding was usually from the Older Americans Act, but they now receive money from a number of sources.

One of the single most important functions of these centers is their meal programs, which provide a hot lunch at midday. These low-cost meals are not only nutritionally sound, but also provide an opportunity for socialization by the participants. The importance of this program for the single elderly cannot be overestimated. Not only does it provide a balanced diet for a person who might find meal preparation bothersome, but it establishes human contact for those whose lives might otherwise be devoid of daily human contact.

Well-funded centers may provide transportation to and from their building. Meal costs are often quite low, and even free if they are funded by the 1972 Nutritional Program for the Elderly and the 1978 Amendments to the Older Americans Act, although these funds are gradually being phased out with recent budget cuts.

## MEALS ON WHEELS

While senior centers may provide a reasonably priced midday meal for the ambulatory, the Meals on Wheels program delivers food directly to the home. This hot lunch is nutritionally sound and usually includes the makings for a cold evening meal as well. Delivery time is also a period of limited social contact and a check on the recipient's well-being.

This very successful program began in 1945 as a strictly voluntary effort. At present meals are still delivered by volunteers, but part of their cost may be defrayed by government, private or community money. The recipient's charge for the delivery usually runs from $5 to $18 a week, although meals delivered under the Federal 1978 Home Delivered Meals Program are free. In some areas, a Kosher Meals on Wheels program is also offered.

There is wide variation in the availability of this program and its cost. To determine if a program is available in your area, contact the nearest senior citizen's center or your local Visiting Nurse service.

## TRANSPORTATION SERVICES

Senior transportation services also vary widely in availability. In some areas they simply consist of a few volunteers, using their own cars, who make trips for seniors to the local shopping center on an intermittent basis. In other areas they consist of scheduled bus runs to medical centers, shopping centers and downtown areas. The extensive programs may also include dial-a-ride vans with wheelchair access and runs to distant hospitals for medical treatments. Some major metropolitan areas may do as little as offering seniors discount tickets on their mass transportation systems.

Transportation services are usually free, but a contribution is requested. Many of these programs were begun with federal funds, but budgetary problems have decreased money from this source. State departments on aging and local contributions are the primary source of funding for transportation programs at this time.

## TELEPHONE REASSURANCE PROGRAMS

Loneliness, the fear of falling or being struck ill, is often enough to drive the single elderly from their homes. Telephone reassurance calls made on a daily basis can do a great deal to alleviate the fear of lying helpless without hope of help. The calls are made by concerned relatives, friends, volunteer groups or paid services.

A good example of a viable volunteer telephone reassurance network is the "Are You O.K.?" program in Stamford, Connecticut. O.K. was started in 1985 by Kay Pfaff after she learned of two deaths of the elderly in her town that went unreported for days. She began the program in her own home, but it was soon transferred to Stamford Hospital because of increased usage. The hospital's switchboard was quickly overburdened by the task, and the Red Cross took over the program. At present several hundred volunteers, working for a dozen large corporations, make daily phone calls to more than 225 Stamford residents. If they do not receive an answer to their initial call, they try a backup contact with a friend or relative. If necessary, they call 911 or a social service agency to make personal contact with the elder.

These phone calls have a triple function. They check on the physical well-being of the person called, they allay fear in the elderly living alone and they provide a moment of socialization. For the single person living alone, this may be their only human contact during the day. A single call of a few minutes' duration can somewhat reduce the loneliness so many of these people suffer.

## EMERGENCY RESPONSE SYSTEMS

A telephone reassurance call is of no immediate help if you can't reach the phone. And those who have fallen and are unable to rise, or are critically ill, may not be able to make the necessary phone call for aid. Although not a community service, commercial emergency response systems of various kinds fulfill this need.

There are three basic kinds of response systems, all of which are triggered either by self-contained pendants worn around the neck or by small units worn on the belt. Once activated, these systems cause the house phone to dial a predetermined list of phone numbers, to directly contact the hospital in the system or to signal the system's monitoring center.

Lifeline, the oldest of the systems, connects directly to a response center at a local participating hospital. Another system connects the emergency signal to their national monitoring center. Costs vary widely. Medicare, Medicaid or private insurance plans do not pay for these services.

In obtaining an emergency system, care should be taken that the company provides the pendant or belt device. Equipment can be costly if purchased, so a lease arrangement is often more practical, but will run from $50 to $75 per month. Response time is an important factor, but the providing company must assure its users that the system will work without voice activation. A fall or stroke may leave an elderly person confused or unable to speak, and he or she may be able to trigger an alarm device but not be able to carry on conversation.

For further information contact:

Medical Alert
AT&T Special Needs Center
2001 Route 46
Parsippany, NJ 07054
800-233-1222

Lifeline
Lifeline Systems
One Arsenal Market Place
Watertown, MA 02172
617-923-4141

## CHORE SERVICES

One of the most significant reasons the retired leave their homes after years of occupancy is difficulty with routine maintenance. Cleaning leaves from rain gutters and replacing storm windows with screens in older homes are typical tasks that are difficult and dangerous for the elderly. For apartment dwellers or home owners, other heavy tasks can pose nearly insurmountable obstacles. Yard work, floors and window washing, trash disposal and routine repairs have forced many people into group housing merely because these services are routinely provided there.

Realizing that routine chores can be a problem for the elderly, the Visiting Nurses in Dallas, Texas, formed a program called Independence Plus. For a fee of $10 an hour they will arrange housekeeping, homemaker services or maintenance and chore service for their elderly participants. The New York Foundation for Senior Citizens offers a home repair service for those on a limited income. The Wisconsin plan, mentioned earlier, provides chore service as part of its program to keep people in their homes. Several of the Canadian provinces, which utilize a case manager system for the care of their elderly, routinely provide chore service when necessary.

While there are thousands of profit and nonprofit home health care and homemaker agencies throughout the country, few provide chore service. Homemakers, and certainly not health personnel, do not do heavy housekeeping, much less lawns. This type of activity is often performed by friends and relatives of the elderly and, in rare instances, by formal programs of a voluntary nature. The need for these services is not nearly so acute for apartment dwellers, where building management usually provides adequate maintenance.

## ELDERHOSTEL

Life can't be all chores. The senior years are a time to travel and learn. Elderhostel is a program that provides mental stimulation tied to bargain travel arrangements. They are located at 75 Federal Street, Boston, MA 02110. This group works with more than 1,000 colleges in the United States and 37 foreign nations. They offer one-to three-week not-for-credit mini-courses in a host of topics ranging from the mystery novel to the volcanoes of Hawaii.

Elderhostel was started in 1975 by Martin P. Knowlton, a teacher, and David Biano, a university administrator. In the first year they escorted 225 seniors to five New England colleges for their week-long programs. By 1990, more than 150,000 people a year were enrolled in the program.

Participants must be at least 60 years old and pay approximately $235 a week, excluding transportation, which includes the course, room and board at the college and the use of swimming pools, tennis courts and other campus amenities. The educational level of attendees ranges from Ph.D.s to high school dropouts.

# HEALTH SERVICES

## KATE CARES FOR ALLEN, BUT WHO HELPS KATE?

It was Allen's pride that was driving Kate up the wall. It had gotten to the point where each day was a struggle and she didn't want to get out of bed in the morning.

They had both known that when they reached their seventies problems might occur and their health could deteriorate. Allen's late-onset diabetes had been their first obstacle. With their doctor's help, they had learned to control that condition with diet, weight loss and oral medication. It was Allen's stroke that devastated them. His right-side stroke, which affected his left side but left speech unimpaired, had only partially incapacitated him. He had responded well at the rehabilitation center and was home within a month. His movements were slightly restricted, and he walked with an awkward gait that created a tendency to fall. However, he was stubbornly determined not to allow this condition to change his life.

It was Allen's constant struggle against his condition that made Kate's life difficult. If he had to go to the bathroom at night he would slip from bed without awakening her and often fall. He would fall at odd times during the day, always refusing to ask for Kate's help beforehand. Kate was a tiny woman and helping Allen after a fall was a physical strain. She tried to minimize this problem by constantly watching him.

Although Allen had only minor short-term memory loss, this, combined with the fall trauma, created mild confusion. Kate's life took on a nightmarish quality. Grocery shopping and errands were travesties. She couldn't take him with her and leaving him alone was dangerous. She knew that her energy was waning, and she seriously considered placing Allen in a nursing home. She couldn't see any other answer.

The elderly taking care of the elderly is not an uncommon problem, and it often has tragic consequences for all concerned. Kate can drive herself until she is in physical and mental jeopardy, or she can place Allen in a nursing home—a placement that he does not necessarily need at this point.

If the community in which this couple lives has a decent network of elderly services, the answer for Kate might be . . .

## RESPITE CARE

A few hours a day, or a week's vacation from time to time, would remove Kate from her constant need to attend to Allen. Such an arrangement might be her salvation and keep Allen from a nursing home admission. Respite care might be arranged from several sources:

Board-and-care facilities (rest homes), often offer temporary arrangements to those residents who qualify for this level of care with protected oversight (see Chapter 15 for a full discussion of these custodial establishments).

Skilled nursing homes that have a vacancy, or that are reserving a bed for future use, might admit a patient for several days or a week.

Home health care agencies can provide around-the-clock temporary care in the home with the appropriate level of personnel.

Adult day-care centers offer daily programs that would be appropriate for Allen's physical and mental problems. This would result in several hours a day of respite for Kate. (See following section.)

Active support groups often form care co-ops to trade respite hours with each other.

## SUPPORT GROUPS

There seems to be a support group for nearly every known affliction. These organizations vary in efficiency, knowledge and availability. The Alzheimer's Association is a good example of an active and sophisticated support group. They have a national office, 70 Lake Street, Chicago, IL 60601, with state chapters throughout the country and local chapters in most populous counties.

Support group meetings can provide socialization for the caregiver with others in the same circumstances. These groups are also a prime source of information as to the availability of other useful services.

## ADULT DAY CARE

It is estimated that there are at least 2,100 adult day-care centers in the United States. These are not to be confused with senior centers. They are occasionally located in the same building, or even operate under the organizational umbrella of a senior center, but their mission is distinctly different. An adult day-care center offers health support, protective oversight and personal care in addition to recreational activities and the balanced meal offered at the senior center.

Adult day care operates on a weekday schedule, and the staff usually consists of social workers, nurses, aides and often various therapists.

An adult day-care center should provide health monitoring, personal care, protective oversight, a balanced meal, transportation to and from the center and recreational activities appropriate to the clients' physical and cognitive abilities. Services may also include medication supervision, rehabilitation, occupational therapy, skilled nursing care, social services, podiatry and psychiatric evaluation.

These centers may be publicly or privately owned. On a national average they cost $35 a day, including the meal and transportation. In many areas, where funding is available from other sources, these fees are on a sliding scale indexed to ability to pay. Thirty-five percent of all day-care fees are paid by Medicaid (a joint federal-state entitlement program for those of low income and few assets).

Adult day care is a growing field, and many of the newer units specialize in the care of specific groups such as Alzheimer's patients or the visually impaired. A few of the centers, which are affiliated with hospitals or nursing homes, offer extensive rehab and skilled nursing services as well as the other programs.

Unfortunately, there are no federal regulations concerning these centers, and state oversight in sketchy. The Intergovernmental Health Policy Project in 1989 reported the following for state regulations of adult day care:

states that had standards for certification      6
states that had standards for funding only      6
states that had standards for licensing         22
states that had no standards                    16
(See Appendix for a state-by-state listing.)

The National Institute of Adult Day Care states that regulations are good to excellent in the states of California, New York, New Jersey, Maryland and Virginia.

This lack of adequate regulation and inspection means that prudent care must be taken in the selection of any adult day-care facility. In making a choice, watch for the following:

- Avoid those located in private homes. This type of cottage industry will provide a meal, lots of television watching and little else of any value.
- Try to locate a center sponsored by an organization or group whose reputation is known to you. Examples of these are centers located in senior centers, affiliated with a local church or other charitable organization, or that have a board of directors whose reputations are familiar. This will not guarantee the success of their program, but it might at least indicate that they are reputable and have the proper intent.
- Check whether one staff member is provided for every eight participants.
- Ascertain that an assessment and care plan is made for each person admitted to the program.
- Ask about emergency procedures and arrangements.
- Look at their calendar of daily activities to see whether they are appropriate for the individual you are attempting to place.
- Check the daily menu and compare it to what is actually served.

The most revealing insight into any center is your observation of the other participants. Are they involved or are they lethargic? Does the staff interact with the participants, or are they "sitting" their charges?

# HOME HEALTH CARE AGENCIES

Medicare and private cost-containment insurance policies are presently structured to encourage hospitals to discharge patients as soon as possible. This means that many individuals often arrive home weak and in need of further stabilization or rehabilitation. Skilled nursing on a part-time basis may be necessary, along with homemaker service for those who live alone.

The National Association for Home Care estimates that there are more than 5,000 home health agencies in the country. There are probably another 5,000 homemaker agencies. A homemaker can provide light housekeeping, shopping, the preparation of meals, laundry services and companionship. A home health agency provides registered nurses, licensed practical nurses, health aides and others from specialty fields, such as physical and occupational therapists.

## COSTS

If skilled nursing is required, in all but the most complex case an LPN should be adequate. An LPN will cost from $1.00 to $4.00 less per hour than an RN. Keep in mind that if medications are to be administered, injections given or invasive nursing tasks performed, a licensed person (RN or LPN) will be required. Professional nurses will not perform household chores not directly related to the care of their patient. Separate arrangements must be made for general housekeeping.

Aides and homemakers are limited in the nursing tasks they may perform, but if custodial or personal care is all that is needed, their skills would be adequate.

Estimates from a survey by the U.S. House of Representatives Select Committee on Aging give the following costs for home nursing in the United States:

> Registered nurse per hour    $26 to $45
> Home health aide per hour    $11 to $20

In all probability, Medicare will not pay for any of these costs. Medicare regulations are very stringent and will pay for skilled nursing care at home only under very narrow circumstances.

## SELECTION OF AN AGENCY

Choosing the best home health care agency is complicated by the lack of uniform regulatory standards. Although many states license these organizations, few provide inspection programs to monitor the quality of performance. Homemakers operate virtually without supervision.

We have abstracted below some of the questions the National Association of Home Care recommends asking about any agency under consideration:

1. How long has the agency been in business?
2. Does your physician know the reputation of the agency?
3. Is it certified by Medicare? Even if these benefits are not available to your patient, this certification at least indicates that the agency has met minimal requirements.
4. Is the agency licensed by the state?
5. Does it provide a written statement describing all the services it will deliver, along with costs?
6. How does the agency select and train employees?
7. Does a nurse or therapist conduct an evaluation?
8. Is there a formal care plan for each patient?
9. What emergency arrangements does it make?
10. Does it guarantee patient confidentiality?

Do not confuse a home health care agency with a nurse's registry. The registry is an employment agency for nurses and does not offer a complete package of services.

If you feel your patient may be eligible for Medicare benefits, ask the agency you are considering what their success rate is with Medicare approvals. A knowledgeable agency should have a 40% Medicare approval rate.

# WHAT'S REALLY OUT THERE?

## FUNDING PROBLEMS

Many community services are at least partially dependent on income received from state governments. Massive state budget deficits are forcing a reduction in senior programs for 1991 and future years.

At least 20 states have recently reduced spending for their elder programs. North Dakota is cutting the financing of 250 senior centers and some of the money paid to workers who do household chores for the elderly. California is making massive cuts in its meal delivery program. Florida and Arizona are cutting in-home services, while Colorado is scaling back its transportation program. West Virginia and Minnesota are also cutting back on their senior center funding—and other state cutbacks are in the offing.

## FORM OVER SUBSTANCE

The Meals on Wheels program does a good job in most nonurban areas. The network of senior centers has expanded and provides many recreational programs and noon meals to countless seniors. Transportation programs are extensive in some areas and nonexistent in others. Generally speaking, the other senior programs are more form than substance.

Outside of transportation, the two most necessary services seniors require to maintain their independence are chore aid and respite care.

Except for a few shining exceptions, such as the Wisconsin plan and certain effective volunteer groups, chore aid and respite programs simply do not exist. The affluent can avail themselves of commercial lawn and cleaning services and also utilize health care agencies for respite care. These expensive solutions, however, may not be possible for those with even generous pension incomes.

Generally speaking, heavy chores for seniors are more apt to be performed by friendly neighbors or relatives than by any formal group. Although there are presently many community hospitals with vacant beds, formal respite care programs have not evolved. Nursing home bed vacancies are a rarity, and the cost of more than $100 a day is a strain on most retirees' budgets. As a consequence, respite care for an ill spouse or parent is arranged in haphazard fashion, if at all.

Under present budgetary constraints, the federal government has made no move to fill this vacuum, and state governments are reducing or eliminating programs rather than adding to them. As a consequence, many semi-independent seniors are forced from their homes under circumstances in which a little physical aid at modest cost would have allowed them to remain.

# PART TWO

# ASSISTED LIVING

The second-generation elderly have begun to either experience or anticipate the debilitating effects of chronic illness. They may still be in relatively good health, but they have started to restrict their activities. Often, there has been a major restructuring of lifestyle because of the loss of a spouse. Cooking regular meals, keeping a large home (or even a moderate-size condominium) may seem inappropriate to the widowed. The companionship of others may take on greater importance now that the elder is single again for the first time in decades.

It is at this point that many who have migrated to the Sun Belt return to their area of origin to be near family and friends. There is an increased concern over emergency medical response. A home in a retirement village or that winterized cabin on the lake has lost appeal because of these concerns.

As this second generation approaches the age of 75 they know that the risk of falls, strokes and other health problems has dramatically increased. Their eyesight and hearing have declined and perhaps their energy level is a bit less than it had been.

For these and other reasons, these people want a living alternative that is as free as possible from daily encumbrances. They either desire or require the proximity of others for emergency or some other form of care or aid.

# CHAPTER 8

# WITH A LITTLE BIT OF HELP: Accessory Apartments, ECHO Housing, Home Sharing and Group Homes

## SOMEONE NEAR

The housing continuum is not a seamless structure that progresses in a straight line from point A to point B. Unless there is a rapid onset of an acute illness, individuals do not live independently one day and require assisted living the next. It may begin when certain of life's daily requirements, such as routine chores, become increasingly difficult, or when concerns over physical security cause increasing anxiety in those living alone.

It is reassuring and helpful to have more agile people nearby. These other adults, be they family, friends, tenants or housemates, can increase socialization, perform certain housekeeping tasks and maintain a watchful eye on those elderly who may be prone to falls or other physical problems. A housing arrangement that creates this small assistance may be sufficient to allow some elderly to remain in their homes.

In addition to the advantages just mentioned, each of the housing arrangements that follows also has distinct financial benefits over nursing or custodial home placement.

## ACCESSORY APARTMENTS

Also known as in-law suites, mother-daughter apartments, second units or single-family conversions, accessory apartments are self-contained units constructed within a single-family home. They were mentioned in Chapter 2 as a possible source of extra income for those who chose to stay in their own homes. They can work advantageously in either of two ways: as a

78

rental unit that provides extra income for the retired individual, or as a unit occupied by the elderly who need the security and partial assistance of others.

There are 18 million single-family homes in the country of five or more rooms that are occupied by only two people. It is estimated that 1.5 million of these contain a legal or illegal accessory apartment.

## ADVANTAGES

If the elderly person is the homeowner, the rent he or she receives may be quite useful to his or her fixed income. If he or she is the tenant, the rent will generally be far less than what would be charged for an identical apartment elsewhere.

A self-contained accessory apartment allows an independent way of life with the security of others nearby. Rent may be reduced or leases may include provisions that heavy chores are to be done by a younger tenant. The older party may reciprocate by providing such services as baby sitting.

Creation of the apartment precludes the older person from the necessity of moving from the home or allows him or her to remain in a known neighborhood. If children and parents are the occupants, it removes a source of worry, reduces travel time for visiting and still allows the maintenance of separate households.

If either party travels, the property is protected by the presence of the remaining occupant. This is helpful for those elderly ''snowbirds'' who will not have to worry about their home while they are down south for the winter.

Accessory apartments expand an area's supply of dwellings without public subsidy. Since they are constructed within the frame of an existing building, they can be built for as little as $15,000 to $50,000. With only minor exterior change to the home, they provide affordable housing either for the elderly or for younger couples.

## DISADVANTAGES

There are two major problem areas concerning accessory apartments. These concern the neighborhood and the disruption of construction.

Neighbors and municipalities worry about these units for fear they will overtax water and sewage systems. There is also concern that small apartments will eventually lead to a transient neighborhood, increased traffic, and change a predominantly one-family street to a multifamily area with a subsequent devaluation of property values.

Single-family zoning ordinances, and often subdivision restrictions or covenants attached to the property, may specifically prohibit such arrangements.

Towns have met the resistance to these apartments in several ways. Some have forbidden them completely, while others will only allow them in more densely occupied areas. Other towns have permitted the units' construction under severe restrictions: requiring off-street parking, no additional front entrance, no change in the facade and that both parties be over 65, related and that one unit be owner-occupied.

As a consequence, tens of thousands of these units are illegally constructed and occupied each year. Although they may violate zoning ordinances, they usually remain undisturbed unless the neighbors rebel. The unresolved question concerning zoning approval of accessory apartments pertains to their future use. What happens to the unit when the property is sold or the elderly inhabitant dies?

The authors live in a state where recently the number of consumer complaints against home remodelers exceeded those against used car dealers. This brings us to the difficulties of approvals and construction.

If the owner of the home is the retiree, he or she is going to have to deal with the town zoning board, building inspectors, contractors (or remodelers), the homeowners insurance company, the tax appraisers, the prospective tenants, irate neighbors and possibly mortgage lenders.

Creation of an apartment may also move the older owner into another unique world—becoming a landlord.

For an elderly first-time landlord, a host of new problems present themselves. Eviction of an unsavory or penniless tenant is costly, time consuming and fraught with emotional difficulty if they live in the same building. In some states, particularly if children are involved, eviction proceedings can take months. As any landlord will inform you, first appearances can be deceiving. There is no way in which tenants can be screened to weed out all undesirable possibilities.

Although age-related decline in intelligence is minimal even in advanced age, the older mind is less elastic and less ready to face new challenges. It is therefore suggested that if construction of an accessory apartment is an option, it be done while the retiree is still fresh and ready to do battle.

# ECHO HOUSING

Also known as granny flats or elder cottages, ECHO housing (Elder Cottage Housing Opportunity) consists of a small but separate living unit constructed or moved to the same lot as a larger home.

This type of housing is more adaptable to rural or semirural areas where lots are at least 6,000 square feet, large enough to accommodate a main house and a second home of 450 square feet or larger.

There are at least two companies that construct dwellings specifically for this purpose, although a manufactured home or other precut construction could also be used. House trailers are not recommended, as their narrow entrances, doors and halls can become difficult for anyone confined to a wheelchair or who suffers from arthritis or any number of other chronic physical ailments.

ECHO housing has basically the same advantages and disadvantages as accessory apartments. Local zoning laws may be more adaptable to their use in rural areas, but surrounding homeowners are also concerned that zoning approval could lead to developer abuse. Their cost is obviously higher than accessory apartments as they do not utilize the plumbing, heating or support walls of an existing building.

This concept originated in Melbourne, Australia, where small portable homes were provided by the Victoria government for elderly rentals and called granny flats. As the idea moved to England and finally to America, the name was changed to the more acceptable ECHO housing. In their original concept, these homes were destined for temporary use, and when the elderly occupant died or was institutionalized, the unit was moved.

Although the concept of ECHO housing has been promoted in the United States by various advocacy groups, it has not received strong public support. Only a small number of units are actually in use, and there does not seem to be any groundswell of enthusiasm for increased usage. This lack of popularity is probably tied directly to the increase of construction costs, which have made these units somewhat impractical. The Australian model for granny flats kept unit ownership with the government; the housing was rented to individuals and returned for reuse when not needed. Individual creation of an ECHO unit is nearly a contradiction in terms, for after expensive construction, where is the unit returned when it is not needed? The answer, of course, is to place the unit on the rental market. This might attract another elder, but more probably a young couple. It is the fear of this solution that haunts surrounding property owners. While providing housing for an aged parent may be very acceptable to property owners, they are also aware that once constructed and occupied, that dwelling will remain on the property, occupied by the general public, for decades to come. Any general zoning variance that allows for construction of this type of unit also provides a potential loophole for developers to build many undersize units.

A viable ECHO housing program would require a long-term pilot program that owned and rented movable units with a waiting list of applicants. Present funding restrictions, along with the uncertainty of length of use, does not make this a viable public program.

# HOME SHARING

## OWNER SHARING

Shared housing is a living arrangement where two or more unrelated persons occupy the same house or apartment. Each person involved has his or her own bedroom, while other house areas are enjoyed mutually. Payment to the homeowner can be on a rental basis, an equal portion of all expenses or any agreed upon mix, including "in kind" or "barter" services. Partial barter payment may include anything from baby sitting to transportation, housekeeping and heavy chores.

Owner Sharing offers distinct advantages to the older homeowner that are similar to those of accessory apartments, without the cost of creating a separate living unit. The owner enjoys the increased security of having others in the home, and the socialization that their presence affords. The sharing provides either extra income or reduced living expenses. Also, barter arrangements may allow the owner to remain in the home longer than would be otherwise practical. It is also an arrangement that can be utilized in a larger apartment just as easily as in a single-family house.

Historically, sharing traces its ancestry to widows who took in boarders. It differs from those rental situations in that those involved truly share the home and help provide for its maintenance. Ordinary renters occupy a room, possibly with some kitchen privileges, on a fee-for-service basis.

In many instances it is easier for the owner to establish a workable arrangement with a stranger, rather than move in with relatives and adapt to a family situation that may be burdened with years of emotional baggage.

A strict interpretation of local zoning regulations may prohibit lodgers, a word that may or may not fit home sharers.

Moreover, a growing number of municipalities and court rulings have begun to recognize "families of choice," which are often construed to include home-sharing arrangements. This broad legal interpretation would exclude owner-occupied sharing arrangements from single-family-occupancy zoning requirements.

Sharing has distinct advantages to the tenant. It offers a pleasant living accommodation with accouterments that would cost far more in the ordinary rental market. Cost can be reduced even further if a barter arrangement is included. Matches between students and the elderly have provided young persons on limited income affordable housing while also granting chore service to the older owner. Sharing between the elderly also can be viable as new relationships are nurtured and become mutually supportive.

Society benefits from home sharing because it creates new living units without cost, preserves neighborhoods without change and is often an economic answer for those on limited incomes.

By its very nature, home sharing is far more intimate than an ordinary landlord-tenant relationship. The constant contact and interaction can be a source of great difficulty and friction, which can quickly destroy the relationship. It has been found that the primary way to reduce misunderstandings is to have a firm grasp of mutual responsibilities from the beginning. It is imperative that all parties agree on the rules before the sharing begins.

A written agreement should be created and signed by all parties. This document should anticipate as many of the potential problems as possible.

It must contain financial information such as who pays what, as well as other details. All chore and housekeeping duties should be fairly allocated according to need and ability. Meal selection, preparation, clean up and time served should be agreed upon before the arrangement takes effect. Visitors, pets, sound levels for stereos and televisions and smoking are only a few of the many details to be considered and agreed upon at an early date.

It is impossible to reduce all the day-to-day details of a living arrangement to a written document. However, if the important details are agreed upon, the minor ones are more likely to fall into place.

## MATCH-UP SERVICES

The obvious problem with this housing opportunity is finding the right compatible individual(s) to share with.

Many sharing arrangements occur naturally through mutual friends or word-of-mouth. An example might be two recent widowers who are members of the same church group. During casual conversation or through friends, they realize that their mutual needs might be satisfied through a home-sharing arrangement. Strangers desiring this alternative may be introduced through a commercial or nonprofit match-up service.

There has been an astounding growth in match-up shared housing programs. In 1981, 50 were identified; in 1988, their number approached 500 in 43 states, two in Australia, one in England and nine in Canada. Thirty-six percent of the people using shared housing are elderly, and two-thirds of these are women. Almost half the programs are in urban areas, with California's 51 the largest number in any single state.

The Shared Housing Resource Center of Philadelphia (6344 Greene Street, Philadelphia, PA 19144) is a national clearinghouse that can provide information concerning identification of individual match programs or give start-up help in originating a group. This center was established in 1981 by Gray Panther activist Maggie Kuhn.

Philadelphia Match is an example of a typical nonprofit group that provides a match service. This group, sponsored by the National Shared Housing Resource Center of Philadelphia, receives funding from the Episcopal Community Services Fund, the Philadelphia and Pennsylvania Departments of Aging and the United Way. They charge a $5 registration fee and a $20 fee if a match is made.

Philadelphia Match's procedure is similar to that utilized by countless similar groups throughout the country. Upon registration, the following procedure is initiated:

1. Applicants complete an extensive application along with a list of likes, dislikes and expectations concerning sharing.
2. References are checked and the home to be shared is viewed. All applicants to the program are screened to make sure they are appropriate.

3. Interviews between potential prospects are arranged.
4. After a mutual decision has been reached by housemates, the organization helps to prepare the Home Sharing Agreement.
5. Staff members work with both parties to make sure that their needs are met and that they have reasonable expectations concerning the arrangement.

## PROBLEMS IN MATCHING

Project Homeshare, founded in 1953 in Hartford, Connecticut, is the oldest match-up program in the country. This project works on behalf of elderly persons desiring tenants, and it follows the same basic procedures as Philadelphia Match. Unfortunately, it has discovered a difference in expectations between the homeowner and the tenant. While the owner desires a long-term relationship, the tenant is apt to be in midlife, going through a divorce, career change or other crisis, and is looking for a temporary solution to a housing problem. As a consequence, the average match lasts only a year or less. A constant revolving door of tenants can be extremely upsetting to an elderly owner.

Other match-up programs report that owners sometimes resent sharing certain prized possessions, while tenants are unhappy with restraints on favorite pastimes or life-styles. Matches between college students and elders seem to work, while those that pair the elderly with single parents have often run into difficulties. Single parents seem to do better when they share with other single parents. In those instances they often establish mutually supportive friendships.

## GROUP-SHARED RESIDENCES

Group homes differ from shared housing in that none of the residents owns the dwelling. They are a group of individuals who have chosen to live cooperatively and to participate equally in the care, financing and maintenance of the dwelling. The house is owned by a public or private agency rather than an occupant.

The average size of a group-shared residence is eight people. Eighty percent of the homes serve only the elderly. Forty-seven percent of the group homes are in urban areas, 38% are in the suburbs and the remaining 15% are located in rural areas. The average resident is a female in her seventies who is in moderately good health.

Group-shared residences should not be confused with board-and-care establishments or certain types of enriched housing (often called sheltered or assisted housing) run by state or philanthrophic organizations. Although board-and-care housing may have a home-like atmosphere, it also has professional management that runs the dwelling and provides protective oversight to the residents. Board and care will also provide professional help with activities of daily living and accept residents who are not fully self-care. This housing alternative is covered extensively in Chapters 15 through 17.

Group-shared homes are occupied by individuals who are basically in good health. They may need assistance to perform certain tasks but are able to contribute in some way to the maintenance of the home.

## THE COTTAGE PLACE

An excellent example of a group-shared residence is the Cottage Place in Ridgewood, New Jersey. This large Victorian home in the New York City suburbs has a screened-in porch, a sunny eat-in kitchen and bedrooms for 12 elderly women and two men. The house is owned and managed by the Unitarian Society of Ridgewood, whose goal is to provide elderly residents with privacy yet responsibility.

Individual rooms are decorated according to the taste of the occupant, and each resident has tasks appropriate to his or her ability. Some set the table, others water plants, sort mail or serve meals to those who are ill.

According to the Shared Housing Resource Center, the Share-A-Home project in Winter Park, Florida, founded in 1969, is the oldest group-shared residence program in the country. Originally formed to help 20 residents, the group now owns 10 homes with 125 members. The Share-A-Home Association owns the homes and leases them to each group, which makes its own rules and levies costs. The groups often hire staff to help with cooking, transportation and other duties.

Group home residents continue their arrangements far longer than individual matchups for three reasons: (1) virtually all group homes require a residency trial period to weed out malcontents or those just not suited for this type of living; (2) since ownership is not involved, no single individual has a proprietary interest; (3) the very nature of group living requires a more permanent commitment than the temporary one-on-one matchup.

For those individuals willing to live with and cooperate with others, a group home is an excellent alternative. The individual cost is moderate, but the combined residence income is sufficient to allow the group to enjoy an excellent standard of living.

## PROBLEMS WITH GROUP LIVING

While it is unlikely that two or three individuals sharing a home will cause neighbors concern, the very words "group home" set off alarms. Surrounding property owners often have a vision of hippy communes, a prison halfway house or worse. Establishing a group in a stable neighborhood requires an extensive public relations effort by the sponsor to allay these fears. Without such a campaign, legal obstacles may doom the residence before the first occupant moves in.

Although a group home may be created for low renovation costs, perhaps adding only another bathroom or two, the cost of real estate purchase is still high. It is this initial start-up cost that has limited the number of group homes in operation.

Organizations that sponsor these homes are generally aware of the necessity for resident decision-making, as well as the pitfalls of too much democratic discussion. Most group homes set aside a time each week for a residents' meeting, but this forum can become squabble time if undirected. It is highly recommended that any group home have an outside moderator to aid in focusing discussions and to provide professional advice.

## CONCLUSION

Accessory apartments can be an answer to security, economic, and possibly heavy chore problems for the elder-owner. However, their creation can cause zoning, tenant and construction problems that can consume time, energy and money. This alternative works best if the elder person occupies the smaller unit, with a younger family member in the remainder of the house. Zoning approval is still the major obstacle to this concept. Towns and neighbors do not fear the elderly occupying a small apartment; it is their fear of what happens to that newly created apartment in the future that stalls zoning permission.

ECHO, or elder, cottages are an expensive but satisfactory solution to elderly housing in rural areas. The full ECHO concept is far from realization because of a lack of available rental units and a suitable clearinghouse to facilitate their reuse.

Home sharing, either with an individual or with a group, expands the stock of existing homes and is economically beneficial to all concerned. This living arrangement can provide a built-in support group but requires a true commitment to communal living. It is unfortunate that even the best match programs report individual sharing arrangements of only 7 to 12 months' duration, with only 8% lasting more than two years.

# CHAPTER 9

# CONGREGATE HOUSING: Making Life Easy

## IT'S ALMOST INDEPENDENCE

### FLOEN, 80

Floen had always been grateful that her son, Ralph, had been far too young to serve in World War II, a bit young for Korea, and too old for Vietnam. She was not sure that she was terribly grateful that he had married Clarissa. Her daughter-in-law appeared dutiful. After all, she had taken Floen into her home after John's death when the rheumatoid arthritis made it difficult to continue living alone.

It was the slightly condescending attitude and veiled remarks of personal ownership that surfaced when the two women were alone that undermined the relationship. Floen felt trapped. Her deteriorating eyesight and stiff joints had caused her to surrender her driver's license. Living alone, with the daily chores that were now hard to perform, had become increasingly difficult, until they reached near-impossible proportions. She could not live alone, and she was not happy living in Clarissa and Ralph's home. Was there any answer?

One Sunday, Clarissa and Ralph went to a local restaurant for brunch. Floen declined, and as she flipped through the Sunday papers, the advertisement for the Maples Retirement Apartments caught her eye. She read the ad carefully and within minutes was on the phone to their sales office.

The Maples was a private congregate complex. On the following Tuesday the sales office arranged for its van to pick up Floen at the house. She was driven to the retirement apartments and given the grand tour.

The Maples move-in specialist began by showing Floen several model apartments. The one-bedroom with efficiency kitchen fit into her budget. She noted that the monthly fee included all utilities except for cable television and telephone. The apartment was equipped with an emergency call system in the living area and bath. The bathroom also had the appropriate grab bars and other safety devices.

Floen learned that her monthly rental fee included weekly linens and housecleaning, and one meal a day in the dining room. The apartment's transportation van made daily trips to a local shopping mall and medical center. She was shown a recreation calendar that indicated a number of events planned by the professional recreation director.

A discussion with the project manager revealed that her physical limitations were within their guidelines.

Floen left the Maples with a profound sense of relief. This type of congregate living provided just the right amount of support she needed to live on her own. She also realized that the communal meals and recreation events would force her to mingle with the other residents and help her to handle her loneliness.

The only remaining problem was to break the news of her move to Clarissa and Ralph. She somehow felt that her daughter-in-law would be greatly relieved.

# WHAT IS CONGREGATE HOUSING?

As with so many living arrangements in the senior housing continuum, congregate housing is known by several names. You can find it listed as assisted-living retirement homes, senior residences, carefree retirement living, senior communities and rental retirement communities.

Senior congregate housing is a living arrangement in which many housekeeping and other services are provided by a professional staff. These units are usually high-rise rental units, although condominium ownership is occasionally found, as are garden-style buildings. One or more meals a day in the communal dining room are included in the monthly fee. The common areas include recreation rooms, laundries and other service centers. Housekeeping and linens are often provided and transportation vans are usually available. Personal and property security are stressed, and emergency services with 24-hour-a-day response are universally provided. The living units can range in size from semiprivate rooms to two-bedroom suites and cottages complete with kitchens.

There is a wide range of cost for these living arrangements. At the lower end of the scale are federal, state and locally subsidized programs, which charge a portion of Social Security or Supplemental Security Income benefits, and philanthrophic organizations, which base fees on the ability to pay.

Profit-making corporations provide the same services with extra amenities for fees that run from $1,000 to $5,000 a month.

Residents should be generally in good health, although they may suffer from age-related restrictions or a nondebilitating chronic condition. It is common practice for the congregate facility to require a doctor's statement from the resident that these facilities are adequate for his or her needs. Residents may use walkers or wheelchairs, but they should be able to perform most ADLs (activities of daily living) independently.

Congregate housing is not licensed or inspected by state or federal authorities, although it may receive financial support from a governmental body. It is often sponsored by religious or fraternal organizations. There has been a great deal of recent activity in the private sector as independent developers construct and manage this type of housing.

# THE HUD PROGRAM

The Housing and Community Development Act of 1978 authorized the Department of Housing and Urban Development (HUD) to provide some housing, and nonmedical support services, for the elderly and handicapped. The budget cuts of the Reagan administration caused it to be scaled back to a pilot program. Only 68 congregate programs were eventually funded to service 3,000 people. This Congregate Housing Service Program was required to serve meals and to work with residents and existing social service programs in their respective areas.

In addition to funding problems, the program ran into two other major conflicts. In a report to the Senate Special Committee on Aging, HUD reported that the local social service agencies it was required to interact with were often too fragmented to provide the services the residents required. Since HUD was required to serve meals under the provisions of this program, an area in which it lacked expertise, HUD came into conflict with the Department of Health and Human Services.

Although the program has had difficulties, an evaluation of results at the Hebrew Rehabilitation Center for the Elderly in New York City found that congregate residents in the program required far less nursing home institutionalization than did elders in the general community.

President Bush and HUD Secretary Jack Kemp as part of their HOPE (Housing Opportunity for People Everywhere) program have proposed $10 million in vouchers to pay for senior services, and $34 million in additional elderly housing assistance in 1991. This would serve an additional 1,500 frail elderly and allow them to live independently and not enter nursing homes. The minute federal congregate program of 3,000 elderly and HOPE's 1,500 still total only 4,500 people.

# STATE PROGRAMS

The states have tried to make up for the shortfall in the federal government's senior housing program. Massachusetts has funded more than 50 congregate homes, which are rented to those with a yearly income of less than $15,000. Monthly charges are set at 25% of the applicant's income.

Many other states, while not directly constructing or maintaining congregate housing, do subsidize programs or run pilot programs through their departments of aging. However, present funding problems have caused most state housing agencies, whether working alone or with local housing authorities, to devote their efforts and limited funds to low-cost housing in general. Although a great many of these units consist of senior housing, they have been unable to develop many congregate programs.

The New York State program, Enriched Housing, provides for supervised congregate living in apartment settings. In this program, residents share apartments that are under the management of professional supervisors. One meal a day is eaten together, and the ingredients for two other meals are provided. Necessary transportation is provided, and a staff member is on duty 24 hours a day in the event of an emergency. Fees are on a sliding scale according to income. Unfortunately, this is a limited program.

Another limited, although innovative, program is a private Connecticut project where primary real estate financing was obtained from a state housing authority at a below-market interest rate. The city of Middletown housing authority also granted a partial abatement of real estate taxes. In return, the private developer agreed to put a cap of 5% a year on rent increases or the CPI rate of inflation, whichever was greater. Although the congregate units rented for $1,400 to $1,600 a month, 20% of the units were reserved at a sliding scale rate for those whose income did not exceed $27,000 per year.

In the above congregate project, six months after opening only half of the regularly priced units were rented, but all of the reduced-rate apartments were occupied, with long waiting lists.

Interesting pockets of opportunity exist throughout the senior housing continuum. These projects are often only partially funded by state and local authorities or may have received only tax abatements. Their existence is often not widely advertised because of the small number of units involved. The secret is to discover them and aggressively pursue admission.

Each state department of aging will have individuals or a small department that works with senior housing. State and local housing authorities are also involved in some manner with senior housing. Telephone calls to identify and speak with the proper individuals are time consuming but often can be rewarding. Your local agency on aging may also have information about housing opportunities.

# RELIGIOUS AND FRATERNAL ORGANIZATIONS

Religious and fraternal organizations operate some of the most attractive and affordable congregate housing in the country. Many of these projects are multilevel in the type of care they offer. In many instances they overlap with custodial or board-and-care housing since they often provide protective oversight.

Applicants often have difficulty in obtaining admission to one of these facilities because of long waiting lists and the necessity of a prior relationship with the organization.

Officers and leaders of religious or fraternal organizations that you have direct or indirect relationships with should be contacted concerning senior housing. Many of these groups, while perhaps not operating such programs in your state, may have opportunities in other parts of the country.

# PRIVATE CONGREGATE HOUSING

## ENTER HYATT HOTELS

Although private developers have been involved with senior congregate housing for a number of years, the recent entry of a Hyatt Hotel subsidiary into the field is a sign of its new importance. In the late 1980s, Hyatt formed a subsidiary corporation specifically for this type of development. Classic Residences by Hyatt began by constructing units in Chevy Chase, Maryland; Reno, Nevada; Dallas, Texas; Teaneck, New Jersey; and Monterey, California.

The facilities usually include from 150 to 350 independent-living apartments; some buildings have assisted-living units; and all have congregate facilities and amenities. The prices range from $1,550 to $4,000 per month, depending on unit size and geographic location. Hyatt intends to continue building four to five projects a year, some of which will eventually be franchised.

Each project contains one- and two-bedroom units, each with full kitchen. There is a restaurant-style dining room that serves two meals daily, scheduled transportation and weekly linen and housekeeping services. A main living room, beauty and barber shop, wellness center, craft and activity center, library and reading room are also included.

The offerings by this major corporation are not dissimilar from those made by other private projects.

## A BRIEF SURVEY OF CONGREGATE OPTIONS

A brief survey of other newly constructed senior congregate housing reveals a number of similarities:

Most of the projects surveyed required a doctor's health certificate for entry, and many asked for a financial statement. They were very concerned that the health needs of the resident could be met by this type of congregate living.

The private projects universally provided linen and housekeeping services, a luxury seldom found in the subsidized government housing.

Scheduled transportation was always offered, with special trips arranged at additional cost.

Emergency call bell systems were always installed, with 24-hour coverage.

Some congregate facilities offered three meals a day, although the prevailing mode is to provide one meal a day. Most have kitchens, but some do not.

Less than one-third of the surveyed projects provided assisted-living units (often called barrier-free units). These units, which often have a microwave instead of a standard oven, provide nurse's aide coverage for part-time help with ADLs.

Most projects required from one to two months' security deposit with the first month's rent.

Each complex offered extra amenities such as recreation programs, cocktail parties, craft rooms and libraries.

## COSTS

The Hyatt Classic Residence fee range of $1,500 to $4,000 per month is the prevalent scale for these private projects. Of the projects surveyed, the lowest was $1,400 per month for one individual in a one-bedroom unit. The highest was $4,800 for one individual in a two-bedroom unit with three meals a day.

The cost for a second person in the unit ranges from a low of $200 to a high of $750 per month.

In those instances where assisted living was provided, the costs were higher because of the increased level of care.

# Choosing a Congregate Facility

The main problem in obtaining this type of housing is financial. There are just not enough subsidized facilities to service the need. Nonprofit congregate apartments with sliding fee scales usually have long waiting lists. Private projects, with their resort-hotel luxuries, are lovely—and expensive.

Paradoxically, the very advantages of congregate living—communal meals, socialization and emergency call system—are actually drawbacks for some independent individuals who have lived for decades in their own homes or apartments. Congregate living, by its very nature, requires the surrender of privacy and adherence to group rules. This loss must be measured against other gains.

## Two Things to Watch For

The most common complaint made by residents in congregate apartments is their loss of kitchen facilities. While prepared restaurant-style meals are helpful, those without kitchens often wish they could prepare one or more of their own meals each day. Many congregate apartments do have kitchens, and we recommend that you insist on this if the resident is capable of preparing any food.

Although congregate living is assisted living, it is not a skilled nursing home. Some complexes do offer assisted-living apartments where part-time health aides are available, three meals a day are offered and perhaps protective oversight is installed for drug regimens. It is highly recommended that this type of service be available when the congregate apartment is selected.

## Deceptive Health Care Promises

It is unfortunate, but some of the private congregate residences market their health care deceptively. A cursory reading of their attractive brochures, or conversations with sales personnel, would lead you to believe that a large health care staff is on call in the building, poised to rush forward and provide all types of services when required. They also may indicate that nursing homes are available nearby, along with a wellness center, individually tailored health-care options, professionally coordinated home health care, home health aide referrals and the availability of personal care.

A "wellness center" usually consists of a nurse's office, one nurse and an examining room. Your doctor can use that room while the nurse takes your blood pressure. An investigation into the affiliated nursing home will often reveal that a resident has only the privilege of being placed on their waiting list. In some states it would even be illegal to jump the list because of any such "affiliation." Individually tailored health aide referrals, or the availability of personal health care, means that the staff nurse will refer you to an outside home health care agency. This agency will provide fee-for-service care to the resident, which is often expensive.

The only true benefit these so-called ancillary health options offer is that the resident staff will often help to coordinate them. They may also screen the health agency and nursing home for reliability and safety.

## QUESTIONS TO ASK

You have toured several congregate apartment complexes and have found one in a convenient location that fits your pocketbook. The grounds, common areas and units are attractive and well kept. You have sampled the food in the dining room and found it tasty and attractively served. What else do you do and ask?

As always, in any alternative living arrangement, speak with the other residents. If there is any hidden discontent, these are the people who will reveal it.

Ask whether the dining room will provide special diets, such as ordered by your physician. Will they provide tray service to the apartment if the resident is temporarily unable to leave? The main meal of the day should offer a choice of two entrees. Will they provide kosher or vegetarian meals if you so desire?

Talk to the recreation director and look at the calendar of events. A fine rec program might be provided, but does it fit the resident's interests?

Ask about extra charges. What is the cost of meals not included in the monthly contract? Are there any other extra charges of any sort?

Does your lease run for one year? What is the required security deposit? Is there any cap on renewal rent increases? Under what circumstances is the deposit forfeited?

Can you furnish your own unit? Is the unit provided with smoke detectors, emergency call bells, and grab bars?

If the resident has to leave the apartment for a short hospital or nursing home stay, will the monthly rent be reduced?

Make sure the lease states exactly what is included in the monthly fee. It should specify the number of meals provided, utilities, transportation vans and any housekeeping or linen services.

# IT'S STILL A GOOD ANSWER

Congregate apartment living, particularly when used in conjunction with assisted-living units, is a strong candidate for the ultimate answer for elderly seniors. At the sacrifice of some privacy, it provides security and the release from burdensome household duties.

It is unfortunate that funding for public units is so sparse and that successful pilot programs have not been duplicated. Private-sector accommodations, complete with luxury amenities, offer the same services at far greater cost. Only the most affluent can afford these luxury units, but even in this instance one should be wary of misleading health-care claims.

CHAPTER 10

# LIFE-CARE COMMUNITIES: The Continuing Care Retirement Option

## WHAT ARE THEY?

A life-care community provides all the services and amenities that senior congregate housing does, and in addition has guaranteed access to a skilled nursing home. These complexes are sometimes known as continuing care retirement communities (CCRCs), homes for the aging, or just retirement communities. The term most often found in the literature and advertising is "life care." It is important that the term be specifically defined as some other types of alternative housing may represent themselves incorrectly through deceptive advertising.

A continuing care or life-care community is an organization formed to provide housing, support services and guaranteed nursing home admission to people over the age of 62 for a period in excess of one year.

A wide variety of personal and health services can be offered within this definition. Just as the mix of services can vary, so can payment provisions.

Many congregate housing offerings for the elderly will advertise, "Health care plan available," or "Nursing home affiliation without payment of an entry fee," or similar marketing inducements. An investigation into these establishments will reveal that they probably have an arrangement with a health care agency of a fee-for-service basis, and that a nearby nursing home will give "preference" to their residents.

It is true that a community's nursing home need not be physically located on the site with the other living units. However, the nursing home must either be owned by the community or have a contract to provide a certain number of beds to the residents. Anything less is not a guarantee.

96

Many states have stringent waiting-list requirements for nursing homes, to assure Medicaid patients that they receive equal consideration for bed availability. In those states, so-called preference lists would be illegal for Medicare/Medicaid-approved nursing homes. Nursing facilities affiliated with life-care communities are exempt from these waiting-list provisions as they pertain to their own residents.

## DORA T., 77

Irene leaned forward in her wheelchair parked in the atrium of the Shade-view Nursing Home and clutched the hand of her visitor. "My doctor calls it Medicaid, the nurse says Title Nineteen, the social worker talks about going on the state, but I call it welfare!"

Dora sensed the anxiety in her friend's clasp, and returned the pressure. "There must be some mistake. You've misunderstood what they're saying."

"I've been here too long and I'm going to have to stay, but the money has run out. Nearly every penny is gone, and after this month I can't pay the bill."

Dora gave an involuntary gasp, for she knew that as widows they once had nearly identical assets. She tried to laugh. "That's impossible. The house was free and clear when you sold it, and Martin left you the stocks and savings when he died."

"That was before my strokes," Irene said bitterly. "Almost every penny of it is gone. This place costs $140 a day. All the money is gone, and I'm on welfare!"

Dora was still brooding when she arrived home. She stuffed a TV dinner into the oven and continued thinking about her own finances. Her situation was nearly the same as Irene's. After Henry died she had sold the house and bought the condo, with enough money left over to put in safe investments. That extra money had always seemed like her rainy-day fund or an inheritance for the children, but now she wondered.

The ringing phone startled her. She realized it was the first time it had rung in two days. She slowly picked up the receiver. "Yes?"

"You okay, Mom?" her daughter asked. "When you didn't call yesterday, I got worried. You know how hard it is for me to drive over there with the twins. I just wish you'd move into our spare room."

"And I'd probably fall over the twins' bikes and break my hip and turn into the Wicked Witch of the West," Dora laughed. "A burden like me you don't need."

"That's not fair, Ma. You know we love you."

Dora knew that she was loved, and she wanted to keep it that way. She had cared for her ill mother-in-law for five years, and was well aware of the unbidden bitterness that could appear without conscious thought. She had vowed then never to inflict that burden on her own children.

The TV dinner was overdone and dry. Her depression continued, and she knew that was a danger sign. It was time to bring her life back in focus.

When she looked back at it, she always considered it ironic that her bed-ridden friend, Irene, was the one who introduced her into the life-care concept.

"Martin and I had always intended to move into one," Irene said as she handed Dora the literature. "But then I got sick and it was too late. Maybe you won't end up like me."

# A Typical Life-Care Community

## What Dora Found

Dora found that as a resident of the Northeast she had a wide selection from a number of new continuing-care retirement (life care) communities. She discovered that the mature projects were almost always affiliated with non-profit groups, while the newly constructed were often developed for profit by large corporations. Her choice in New York State was limited since that state did not allow life care until 1989.

After a thorough investigation of several communities, she found that she had a choice of one-bedroom apartments for entrance fees that ranged from $60,000 to $125,000, and monthly fees that ran from $781 to $1,400. She knew that she could find lower fees if she widened her search beyond the Northeast to look in areas where land and other costs were lower. Her proximity to her children was an important factor, and she narrowed her selection to those communities located in her state.

The residency agreement that Dora signed when she moved into her apartment provided that the monthly fee could only be raised on an annual basis, and that increase was tied to the rate of inflation as measured by the Consumer Price Index. She knew that her Social Security benefits were similarly indexed, so potential increases did not alarm her.

She was told that her entry-fee refund was based on the "traditional plan." If she should leave the community, or die, either she or her estate would be entitled to a 90% refund, which declined by 2% a month for each month she had occupied her unit.

In order to qualify for entry into the life-care program, Dora had to prove that she was at least 62 years of age and had to present a doctor's statement that she was capable of independent living at the time of entry. She was also asked to submit a complete financial statement.

The administrator told her that she evaluated the financial soundness of applicants by verifying that they had income twice the monthly charges and that other assets exceeded the amount of the entry fee. They also required that each resident carry Medicare Parts A and B and a Medigap insurance policy to cover the deductibles and copayments.

## THE APARTMENT

Dora's entry fee entitled her to occupy an apartment of approximately 700 square feet. Her unit consisted of a smallish but fully equipped kitchen, bath, two closets, bedroom and living room. It also included several other important features for the elderly:

Smoke detectors

Safety grab rails in the bathroom

Thermostat for heat and air-conditioning

An emergency call signal linked to the health center

Garage space

Extra storage in the basement

Doors and halls wide enough for wheelchair mobility

Dora's monthly fee also included one meal a day and all utilities except telephone and cable television. If she needed a plumber or electrician she could call on the maintenance staff at no charge.

Weekly housekeeping was part of the package, and the laundry service provided fresh linens for bath and bed at no additional cost. A self-service, coin-operated laundry for personal items was located a few steps from her unit.

If the medical director felt it was necessary, meals could be delivered directly to her apartment, at additional cost.

## WHAT DORA MIGHT HAVE CHECKED FOR

It is important that the emergency call system not only be located in each room, kitchen and bath included, but that it either have additional buttons located near the floor or be a sash-cord hanging type. It must be assumed that the system will need to be activated after an elderly person has fallen and is unable to rise.

Smoke alarms and fireproof construction are important, and a sprinkler system should also be present.

Electrical outlets should be located 18 inches from the floor to reduce bending and reaching. Kitchen cabinets and work surfaces should not be standard preconstructed units but should be built low enough to be accessible to stooped or wheelchair confined residents. In addition to grab bars, tubs and showers must have nonskid surfaces.

## COMMON AREAS

The retirement community that Dora chose was built against the slope of a gently rolling hill. Attractive landscaping provided pleasant walkways with conveniently located benches. The property was well maintained by an efficient grounds crew.

A greenhouse, outdoor gardening plots and a pitch-and-putt golf course were also available on the grounds. The heated swimming pool was enclosed for year-round use.

The campus-style apartment units were connected to the main building by broad, enclosed hallways. This core contained the administrative offices, dining room and kitchen, library, game rooms, auditorium and recreation center. Near this location was the health center containing assisted-living studios, examination rooms and a skilled nursing facility of 35 beds.

The main building also housed a beauty parlor and convenience store. A full-time recreation director hosted a full calendar of events, ranging from book discussions to bingo.

A transportation van made daily scheduled trips to a shopping mall and was available by reservation for local trips to doctors' offices, dentists or other stops.

Security officers patrolled the grounds and halls while one guard constantly monitored closed-circuit TV screens, whose cameras continuously swept the project's open spaces. Developers of any type of senior housing are well aware that their prospective residents have a deep concern for personal security, and this is usually one of the features they highlight in their marketing material.

## MEALS

Dora's apartment had a kitchen, and she could either drive her own car or take the community van to the supermarket for groceries. Her residency apartment included one meal a day in the common dining room. Most life-care administrators prefer that their residents avail themselves of this meal for several reasons:

It ensures that all residents are eating at least one well-balanced meal a day.

The gathering of residents gives the staff opportunity to see that everyone is present. This acts as an unobtrusive safety check.

The mixing at mealtime precludes complete social isolation.

Dora elected to take her main meal of the day at noon in the dining room. At each meal she had a choice of two entrees or soup and a sandwich. For a slight additional cost she could bring guests to the main dining room or reserve one of the smaller private rooms. If she chooses to eat more than one meal a day in the dining room she will be charged $3 for breakfast and either $4 or $5 for dinner, depending on her choice of a full meal or a sandwich.

# THE HEALTH CENTER

It is the presence of the skilled nursing facility that distinguishes the life-care community from ordinary congregate housing for the elderly. There are other housing alternatives that do not charge any entry fee and that provide all the physical amenities that Dora found in her community. For example, a congregate apartment may have emergency medical services available, but it is always expected that the resident reside independently in his or her unit, or else transfer to a nursing home.

The life-care community, by the terms of its contract, guarantees residents a bed in its skilled nursing home. There are variations in the payment arrangements for nursing home occupancy, but Dora entered a community that provided that all-inclusive plan. Under the terms of this plan, Dora was guaranteed a nursing home bed at no increase in her monthly charges. If the medical director, in conjunction with her attending physician, decides that Dora will never again be able to live independently, the community administrator will request that she give up her apartment. The unit will then be assigned to a new resident. If Dora's stay in the nursing home is only temporary, her apartment will be held for her until she returns.

## WHAT IS A SKILLED NURSING HOME?

A skilled nursing home is equipped to provide 24-hour-a-day licensed nursing coverage for its patients. It is prepared to perform nursing treatments and rehabilitative therapy for those transferred from an acute-care hospital. It also provides long-term care for those suffering from incapacitating or chronic illness that needs round-the-clock monitoring.

All skilled nursing homes are licensed by the state in which they operate. Those nursing homes authorized to accept Medicare and/or Medicaid patients operate under guidelines set by the federal government and are periodically inspected by state teams. Many nursing homes that are part of life-care communities are not Medicare/Medicaid approved. Although this means that they do not fall under federal nursing home standards, they must still operate in compliance with state standards. As a practical matter, state nursing home standards must be equal to the federal standards, and in some instances are far more stringent.

CCRC nursing homes do not avoid Medicare/Medicaid approval in order to skirt regulations, but for financial expediency. Medicare pays such a small portion of nursing home costs (less than 2% of total dollars spent) that its loss is minimal. Title Nineteen of the Older Americans Act (Medicaid) is a federal-state partnership entitlement program that pays more than half of all money spent on long-term nursing home care. However, Medicaid reimburses nursing homes on the basis of a flat daily rate that is far below what is charged to private or self-pay patients. Life-care nursing homes, particularly in the early days of a community, solicit outside patients to fill their unused beds. These self-pay patients defray overhead costs and help fund the nursing home. It is this funding aspect that makes it unattractive for them to accept the lower-paying Medicaid patient.

## ASSISTED-LIVING UNITS

Many of these communities provide assisted-living units for their residents. These small apartments, which are often just studios without kitchens, are usually located in or near the health-care center. Three meals a day are provided, and the nursing staff is near enough to provide protective oversight.

These units are designed to serve those residents who are unable to live independently in their own apartments but who do not need the full coverage of a skilled nursing home. The typical resident is a widow who walks with an assistive device or uses a wheelchair, but can self-transfer. (Self-transfer is the ability to move from a wheelchair to a bed, chair or toilet without assistance.) She is mostly continent, and can perform some ADLs for herself, but needs help with others. She may be able to self-medicate but perhaps needs supervision and reminding concerning her drug regimen.

Assisted living is another stop in the housing continuum. It still provides some independence but also offers the security of immediately available help when it is needed.

## HOME HEALTH CARE

Since the life-care community already has a medical staff in place, it will sometimes offer temporary home health care in the resident's apartment on a short-term basis.

The extent of this service would be minimal, perhaps one or two brief visits during the day. Some for-profit organizations in the field are beginning to form home health care agencies to provide this service to their residents on a more extensive long-term basis. This service is not included in the residency agreement and would be paid for on a fee-for-service basis.

# GUARANTEED HEALTH CARE

It is the aspect of guaranteed health care that makes the life-care community concept so attractive. It is expected that Medicare backed with a proper Medigap insurance policy will pay for an individual's doctor bills and any necessary acute-care hospital stays. If the resident needs nursing home care, a bed is guaranteed, and, under an all-inclusive plan, the costs are covered under the terms of the residency agreement.

## WHY IS THE NURSING HOME SO IMPORTANT?

The cornerstone of a life-care community is its skilled nursing home. The presence of this facility and its guaranteed access form the rationale for the entry fee. The fact that it is a part of the community solves certain problems that are indigenous to the nursing home industry:

Monitoring. As the CCRC matures and more of its residents occupy nursing home beds, there is a continuing surveillance by the community as a whole as to nursing home standards. In the 1960s many unscrupulous operators entered the nursing home field and sacrificed quality to profit. Governmental regulation eventually weeded out most of those individuals, but the scandals created a poor public impression. Against this background, it is difficult for the layman to properly discriminate between the good and the bad.

It is doubtful that the staff of a skilled nursing home located in a life-care community could long survive if it were guilty of abusive care, poor nursing or neglect. The combined outcry by residents would demand immediate correction of deficiencies. After all, even those that are well now know that someday they might be a patient.

Entry is an easier decision. Guilt and anguish are the predominant emotional modes of family members who must arrange for a nursing home admission. Because of the public image of nursing homes, the finality of the decision and the fact that the choice is the last resort, placing a loved one in a nursing home can be torture. These emotional problems are compounded because often the choice of a nursing home must be made in haste.

However, when a resident selects a life-care community, he or she presupposes that a nursing home stay may become necessary in the future. The choice of community has preselected the nursing home. Under these circumstances, the transfer to a nursing home bed becomes a medical judgment only and not cause for a family crisis.

Transfer to the project's nursing home in a life-care community is only a minor relocation. The other patients are at least nodding acquaintances, and the staff is familiar. The facility is part of the community and therefore presents no problem for visitors. This transition is far easier than for members of the general population.

Nursing home occupancy rates. Good nursing homes are hard to find, and the good ones are often full. In the United States the nursing home industry operates at 90% of capacity.

Skilled nursing homes do not operate in a free-market economy. Need does not create expansion, because state governments purposely inhibit their growth. Construction of a new nursing home requires a Certificate of Need. The states curtail the issuance of these certificates for budgetary reasons, because more than 50% of all nursing home patient costs are borne by the state and federal partnership under the Medicaid program. More nursing home beds mean more Medicaid patients, which mean greater expenses for state and federal welfare programs. The states have attempted to relieve the increased pressure for elder care by encouraging home care.

Any state is more apt to give a Certificate of Need to a nursing home constructed as part of a life-care community rather than one open to the general public. Welfare departments know that these beds will either be utilized by self-pay patients or residents. They will not be a financial burden to limited state budgets.

Nursing home costs. These costs are another feature that makes the all-inclusive life-care contract appealing. Under the terms of this type of agreement, the charges for nursing home occupancy will not exceed the resident's present costs. This is a built-in expense cap for participants.

In 1990 the average daily rate for a skilled nursing home in the Northeast was $101.97 per day. The lowest daily rates were found in the South, where an average of $67.89 prevailed. These rates, like all costs in the health care field, rise faster than the annual rate of inflation.

In large urban areas the costs are even higher. The State of New York estimates that the average daily rate for a nursing home in New York City is $160 a day, with only slightly lower fees in suburban Westchester and Nassau counties.

It is only in the last few years that a significant number of private insurance carriers have begun writing policies for long-term nursing home care. These policies are not understood by most insurance agencies and have complicated coverage variables. The cost of these policies is reasonable only if they are taken out during one's third through fifth decade. The cost becomes economically unfeasible if they are written for people in their seventies or older.

It must be repeated that Medicare coverage for nursing home care is constructed so that it does not benefit the vast majority of individuals. Medicare was never intended to be a solution for long-term care costs.

# NOT A BURDEN

Life-care community residents are often powerfully motivated by a desire to never be a financial, physical or health burden on their family or society. They want the guaranteed health care these retirement alternatives offer, as well as the tranquility that comes with the knowledge that they are financially secure.

# CHAPTER 11

# LIFE-CARE PROFILED: People and Places

## THE RESIDENTS

### MORTALITY AND MORBIDITY

These dire-sounding terms describe the frequency of deaths (mortality) and disease (morbidity). Life-care residents have lower mortality and morbidity rates than the general population of their age. The studies are few, but residents seem to have a longer life expectancy than their nonresident peers. They spend fewer days in acute-care hospitals, and their use of skilled nursing home beds is also appreciably less.

Even in life-care communities where nursing home facilities are readily available and where their costs are covered in the contracts, fewer residents occupy beds than those of equal age who live outside the community. Nationally, the number of the advanced elderly (over 85) who live permanently in nursing homes is 20 to 22% of the population. In life-care communities the figures are 15 to 17% for the same age group.

There are several reasons for these differences. A major part of the answer is the self-selecting nature of the residents. Individuals who choose this life-style are concerned about their present and future health needs. This awareness also means that they are more likely to have watched their health in the past, with periodic medical checkups and a moderate life-style. The average resident has a higher level of education and income than the general population, which means that he or she is generally more aware of good health habits and has had the income to pursue those goals.

Life-care communities require a physician's affidavit at the time of admission, attesting that the resident is in good health and capable of independent living. Therefore, this group is generally in better physical condition than others their age.

Several factors in life care itself also help to increase longevity and reduce certain debilitating conditions. Social isolation, poor dietary habits and depression, which can be severe in many of the elderly, are somewhat ameliorated in CCRCs. In addition, if nursing home residency is required, it is only another step in the housing continuum. The patient remains a part of the community. He is near his spouse and is still surrounded by neighbors. The feeling of utter abandonment that can cause extreme depression in outside nursing home admissions is not present to the same degree in these communities.

## WHO ARE THESE PEOPLE?

The average residents are 81 years old and did not enter the community until they were in their late seventies. They arrived directly from their own homes and will live there for an average of 13 years.

Three-quarters of the residents have a college degree and many have graduate degrees. They rate their health as good. Females outnumber males by two to one. For those who do not list themselves as homemakers, the largest single occupational category is business, followed by education, then the professions.

These people are articulate, and they attend resident group meetings. They are concerned with management problems and do not fear voicing their own complaints. They are interested in diverse topics, from recycling to sidewalk and grounds improvements.

# THE COMMUNITIES

The typical community is 14 years old and has 245 residents living in 165 housing units located in garden-style buildings. Some projects have freestanding cottages located on their grounds, while 27% of the communities are in high-rise buildings located in urban areas.

They typically include one meal a day in their basic contract, although three meals a day are available. Usually there is a central core building containing the dining room, health center and common facilities. The living units are connected to the core by a series of interior walkways.

# WHERE DID THEY COME FROM?

The life-care concept has a centuries-long history. Early religious communities were often the final refuge for the old and the ill. The medieval guilds established hostels for their elderly and sick members in order to keep them away from the horrors of the poorhouse.

In 19th-century America the first life-care communities were organized by church groups to provide shelter for their retired clergy. However, these groups gradually absorbed other members of their congregations into their communities. In Pennsylvania, the Friends have been active in sponsoring these organizations for more than a century. Many continuing care retirement communities (CCRCs) in that state still have a Quaker affiliation.

The Methodist, Baptist, Catholic and Episcopal churches also have life-care communities in several states. On a smaller scale, the Board of Benevolence of the Evangelical Covenant Church operates 12 retirement communities throughout the country. Fraternal organizations such as the Masons also sponsor communities.

Prior to 1980 virtually all life-care communities were sponsored by non-profit groups. Nearly half of these groups hired for-profit organizations to manage and to provide food service for their communities.

During this period, half of all CCRCs were located (in order of number) in California, Florida, Pennsylvania, Ohio and Illinois. This distribution is beginning to change as private corporations enter the field.

# EXPLOSIVE GROWTH

There are now nearly 1,000 life-care communities in the United States, or three times the number that existed in 1980. This explosive growth is attributable to the entry of private investors into the field. This trend is just beginning to gain momentum, and it is expected that the numbers will double by the end of the decade.

Prior to 1965 and the passage of Medicare, it was impossible for any profit-making investor to enter the life-care field, because the financial risks of a resident's acute-care hospitalization were too high. Medicare, supplemented by a good Medigap policy, protects the community and resident from most acute-care costs. Private investors also discovered that nursing homes were not only practical, but that in the early days of a project, they were also very profitable. When a community first opens, beds must be filled, and lucrative self-pay patients fill this need and fund the overhead.

It did not take long for the realization to strike developers that while an area's condo sales might be weak, apartments could be successfully marketed if they were tied to congregate living and the health needs of the elderly. Those same elderly also had large amounts of equity in their mortgage-free homes, and so were likely to have the funds to pay for their care.

## ENTER THE FIRST GIANT

In the mid-1980s the Marriott hotel chain formed a subsidiary, Marriott Senior Living Services, to construct and manage life-care facilities. Its first community opened in Haverford, Pennsylvania, in 1989. This corporation feels that its name recognition, real estate background and knowledge of food service and housekeeping will give it the depth to rapidly dominate this new field.

At the Quadrangle in Haverford, Marriott charges an entry fee of $120,900 for a 650-square-foot one-bedroom apartment. The $1,206 monthly fee includes three meals a day. At present, the company is not a leader in the field, but its corporate size and financial resources may well make it a major contender within a short period.

In December 1989, when Marriott, the nation's largest hotel chain, went through a financial restructuring, it sold off many of its fast-food subsidiaries; at the same time, it announced that it would expand its retirement community division and that it expected to have 150 operating within five years.

Interestingly, the future plans of this corporation do not include construction in the Sun Belt. Management feels that states such as Arizona and Florida have been overbuilt with retirement housing, and that people would prefer to live near their former hometowns.

## THE PRESENT LEADER

Life Care Services (LCS) is the nation's largest developer of life-care communities. (It is followed by The Forum Group.) LCS is a wholly owned subsidiary of the Weitz Corporation, a construction company located in Des Moines, Iowa. Weitz, a family-owned company, is the 40th-largest builder in the country. In 1961 it built its first life-care community in Des Moines for a nonprofit sponsor. For the next decade it continued to construct communities, which were turned over to the original sponsors upon completion.

However, Weitz discovered that several of the completed projects foundered after being turned over to the sponsors. In 1971, it formed LCS to provide sophisticated marketing techniques to fill the projects and to perform management functions on a continuing basis. In the 1970s, LCS also offered management services to distressed communities it hadn't constructed and was successful in turning several of these projects around. The next logical step was to develop projects for its own corporation, which it is now doing.

LCS will most likely continue to be an important factor in the life-care field, not only because of its construction background, but because it has had 20 years to develop management depth in the supervision of such projects.

## NONPROFIT AFFILIATIONS

Sixty-three percent of the nonprofit communities are affiliated with another organization, usually a religious or fraternal group. Virtually none of the church-sponsored communities imposes religious requirements.

Affiliation does not mean that the group is financially responsible for the community. Tucked away in the project's marketing literature will usually be a disclaimer statement that reads as follows:

> The Happy Days Retirement Community is affiliated with the X Church, and is a recognized mission of the Diocese; however, the Diocese will have no responsibility for the financial and contractual obligations of the Happy Days Retirement Community.

Members of the sponsoring organization will serve as either trustees or directors of the community. Often the sponsors hire a professional management corporation to perform day-to-day administrative functions of running the community.

Although the sponsors may not have daily contact with the community, they do have a strong moral commitment to the project, and their philosophy and wishes will set the tone for managerial policies.

## AFFINITY GROUPS

A new concept that is presently being used by private developers is to identify the new community with a certain segment of the population. For example, a community might be constructed near a city known for many retired military officers. The developer would attempt to establish a semiofficial or liaison relationship with a local organization of retired officers. The developer would then specifically market development to that particular group. This identification or affinity is only a marketing technique to present the project to a certain homogeneous segment of the retired; the community wouldn't actually be under the aegis of the outside organization.

## JOINT VENTURES

Joint ventures, utilized by both for-profit and nonprofit developers, fall between sponsorship and affinity groups, combining elements of both. One of its elements is a relationship with a well-known organization, which also profits from the sale of units. The financial arrangements vary and may include the sale or lease of land under favorable conditions, bond issues or other types of partnerships.

A perfect example of this type of relationship is the recent interest by colleges and universities in the life-care field. The Marriott Corporation has a partnership with the University of Virginia for a life-care community and expects to build at Notre Dame and Texas A & M as well. The Kendal Corporation of Pennsylvania, which operates two nonprofit Quaker communities in that state, is involved with Darmouth in Hanover, New Hampshire, and expects to build next to the Oberlin College campus in Ohio.

These ventures are attractive to both parties. The developer is able to market to a ready-made group of retired faculty, alumni and those interested in the proximity to a cultural resource—a university. The schools find that these communities can blend in with their campus buildings. The university can enjoy a direct financial return as well as larger alumni gifts and bequests.

## LOOK-ALIKES

Although some elderly congregate apartments make misleading health care promises, some who do seem to offer coverage without entrance fees. These complexes, which charge a monthly rental, seem to offer all the amenities of a life-care community without a large up-front payment.

In appearance, these projects resemble a CCRC. They have a central core containing health facilities, offices and dining rooms. The three types of living accommodations—independent apartments, assisted-living units and nursing homes—radiate off this center section.

Transportation is provided, and they seem to have all the other amenities found in life-care communities.

However, these life-care look-alikes have three basic faults:

1. They are expensive. The cost for single occupancy in a typical one-bedroom unit is as much as $1,750 a month. The charges for the personal care apartments can be more than $3,000 a month. The nursing home charges of $100 a day for semi-private and $115 a day for a private room are competitive.
2. No cap is imposed on future charges. While life-care contracts allow for a yearly increase in monthly charges, these increases are usually indexed to the rate of inflation. A look-alike can raise fees by any amount at the expiration of the lease.
3. Look-alikes cannot guarantee admission to a higher level of care. A CCRC has a financial risk pool generated by the residents' entry fees. A certain percentage of these funds is placed in reserve accounts for future health care. Therefore, whereas a life-care community can reserve beds for residents, a look-alike cannot afford to do that. Any transfer to a higher level of care is dependent on available space.

# A DEFINITE PLACE FOR THE LOOK-ALIKE

A fully structured look-alike has a definite place in the elderly housing continuum. It is appropriate for either direct admission into the personal care units or admission for an individual who has either a deteriorating chronic condition or a terminal illness.

A sound life-care community will not admit residents with either of those health problems. Yet an elderly individual could have any number of health conditions, ranging from congestive heart failure to leukemia, whose immediate prognosis is unknown. These people may be perfectly capable of living independent lives for a period, and then will need greater care as their health deteriorates. Since they are precluded from a life-care community, a look-alike could be a haven for them.

# CONTRACTS AND DISCLOSURE STATEMENTS

States that regulate life-care communities require that any prospective resident be given an information booklet, which is usually called a disclosure statement. A copy of the contract between resident and the community will often be an appendix to this material. This contract may be called a residency agreement, residence and care agreement, continuing care contract, or life-care contract.

Many communities operating in unregulated states find it good business practice to provide similar packages of information to their prospects. Without the information contained in a disclosure statement and a thorough examination of a contract, no informed decision can be made concerning a particular life-care community.

## DISCLOSURE STATEMENT:

This document should contain the following information:

The company. The history of the corporation and its officers and directors should be clearly set forth. Their experience in the life-care field, or related activities, is important to the prospective resident. If a management company has been hired to administer the facility, its experience should also be described.

If the corporation has a church or fraternal affiliation, the extent of that organization's financial liability, if any, should be stated. For-profit corporations may operate through a subsidiary, in which case the extent of the parent company's liability must be determined.

The property. A full description of the property and construction estimates is particularly important if the project is new. Many regulated states require that 50% of the units be sold in a life-care community before construction can begin. Presale usually requires a deposit, which should be placed in an escrow account. The developer should provide a firm timetable in order that future residents do not wait several years to begin their occupancy.

The books. Where disclosure statements are required, their financial information is extensive. In unregulated states this information is often considered proprietary. However, entrance into a life-care community without an examination of its financial condition is the equivalent of purchasing a home without a title search. Audited and certified financial statements should provide the following information:

A balance sheet for the most recent fiscal year

Income and expense statements for the past several years

Estimated income and expenses for the next five years

Reserve funds

Past history of monthly charge increases

If the facility is new, information on the sponsor's financing arrangements

## THE CONTRACT

A life-care contract is lengthy, legalistic and important. No matter how clearly written, it is a document that will require legal interpretation. We recommend that prospective residents compare any contract they are seriously considering with the Contract Checklist in Chapter Twelve, and also have it scrutinized by an attorney.

Involuntary termination of residency is discussed below because this a contractual area where a great many questions arise.

# TERMINATION OF THE RESIDENCY

There are three basic reasons for terminating a residency that seem fairly consistent throughout the industry:

1. Medical reasons, including dangerous or infectious diseases, or for emotionally disturbed behavior that is detrimental to the health and well-being of the resident or others.
2. The failure to pay charges because the resident made unapproved gifts and dissipated assets to the extent that the ability to pay was impaired.
3. Material misstatement of fact(s) on the initial application.

There is a catchall provision that is sometimes seen in these contracts. The wording might be as follows, "Termination can be made for failure to follow the rules of the community including those adopted in the future." On the one hand it is understandable why a community might feel a need to protect itself in this manner; on the other hand it creates a possible booby trap for a new resident. It is doubtful that this paragraph can be removed from the contract, and your only protection is to be comfortable with the people you are dealing with.

Life-care living is congregate living, which entails a close proximity among the residents. Rules—such as limitations on pets, and similar day-to-day items—are obviously necessary. Whether these rules are going to be onerous to any given resident depends on the orientation of that person to the community.

Choosing this type of life-style solely because of physical amenities, price or location would be a serious mistake. These communities, because of their size, are small villages and reflect the personalities of their residents. It would be inappropriate for a free-thinking atheist, whose favorite recreation was wine and cheese tasting, to enter a community sponsored by a Pentecostal church. It is for this reason that affinity groups are often used to attract homogeneous groups to a particular community.

## TERMINATION FOR FINANCIAL REASONS

All communities carefully scrutinize the financial position of a prospective resident. However, as the 1980s so vividly illustrated, even the largest companies can crash, wiping out investors' assets. Life-care management is aware of the possibility and takes it into consideration. They are concerned about individuals who squander their assets or transfer large portions of their assets to children or other relatives to the point where they cannot meet their own obligations. Inadvertent loss of income is treated more leniently.

In the past, when nonprofit homes dominated the field, termination of residency for financial reasons was virtually unknown. The newer for-profit projects are not mature enough yet to have valid data on this problem. However, both nonprofit and for-profit communities should have cash reserves specifically for this type of resident financial problem. Some communities do threaten to terminate residency 90 days after charges are due, but practically speaking, in almost all areas, residents in financial difficulty will be allowed to continue living in the community unless the project itself is foundering.

New York State legislation is quite specific on the subject of financial termination: "A resident shall not be discharged for inability to pay the monthly fee except where a showing of the willful mismanagement of assets needed to pay monthly care fees has been made."

# CHAPTER 12

# LIFE-CARE FINANCES: How Much Does It Cost?

## Only for the Rich?

Some literature describing life care states that it is viable only for the more affluent members of our population. However, since more than 56% of those over 65 own their own homes without mortgages, most of this group can afford the entry fees. These initial costs are partially tied to the price of land in a given geographic area, and therefore will have a direct correlation to the resident's home value in that same area.

Most of the elderly have Social Security, and many have private pensions. The self-employed have often made investments to augment their retirement incomes. Because of these factors, it is estimated that this housing alternatives is within the financial grasp of one-third of our elderly population.

## Life-care Cost Variables

In order to understand the cost structure of any particular life-care community, compare it competitively or evaluate the soundness of any project, one must understand their complicated pricing.

Three resident cost factors must not only be individually rated, but their interrelationship must also be considered:

- Although nursing home entry is always guaranteed, the cost of this service may be completely or only partially included in the contract.
- The initial entry or endowment fee will vary according to the amenities of the project, and the type of unit contracted for; but will also rise or

fall according to the nursing home coverage involved, the amount of monthly charges and the potential refund in the event of death or separation from the community.

- The amount of the monthly occupancy charge is intimately tied to health coverage, the amount of the entry fee and the financial policies of the community.

## NURSING HOME COST VARIATIONS

Dora's life-care community operated on the all-inclusive plan—which meant that occupancy in the nursing home did not create new charges. Not all communities operate in that manner, and may offer alternative arrangements:

Fee-for-service contracts guarantee the resident admission to the nursing home, but the daily rate is an additional charge. The nursing home costs would usually be set at the rate prevailing in the area at the time of admission.

Modified arrangements guarantee a nursing home bed without charge for a set number of days (either per admission, annually or lifetime). When the patient exceeds the allowable days, a daily rate is then imposed which may be in a competitive range or a percentage of the going daily rate (often 80%).

Entry-fee-charge contracts guarantee a nursing home bed without immediate additional charge. If the resident should die or later leave the community, any nursing home fees are deducted from the potential refund of the entry fee.

Which one? Because a nursing home stay can be lengthy (the average patient stays two years) and costly, any community offering the all-inclusive plan will require an entry fee far larger than one granting a fee-for-service contract. It might be possible to invest the money saved on entry fees and apply its investment return against the annual cost of a good long-term-care insurance policy. Consult your financial adviser.

The choice between an all-inclusive versus a modified plan might depend on the financial resources of the resident. However, one of the most agreeable features of the all-inclusive communities is the predictability of future expense. No one can predict the length of a nursing home stay, but unless it is recuperative after an acute illness, it may be lengthy. Modified plans have little to offer unless, once again, there are massive savings in the entry fee.

Entry fee charge contracts are a new concept that are not widely used, and therefore they are difficult to evaluate. If the admission contract guarantees necessary nursing home stays and stipulates a competitive daily rate that cannot exceed the sum total of the entry fee, it may be worth the gamble. These features must be considered in tandem with the amount of the entry fee to be returned before any nursing home stay deductions. In this instance, the community gambles that nursing home costs will not exceed the amount of the entry fee, while the resident gambles that he or she may not utilize this feature of the community at all.

## ASSISTED LIVING

All life-care communities provide a nursing home guarantee, but not all have provisions for home care or assisted living. Our survey of 366, mostly nonprofit, communities revealed that 194 provided some assisted-living units, and a far smaller percentage were involved in home health care for their residents.

For-profit communities are a recent development in the field. These projects are so new that a valid database does not exist. An informal survey of new for-profit projects indicates that they do not have assisted-living units. Their health care leaps from independent congregate living to a skilled nursing home. When questioned about this lack of coverage, administrators said they expected residents to obtain help from the private sector by contacting home health care agencies.

While only 20% of those over age 85 will live in nursing home, half of that age group will require some assistance in basic living. The jump from congregate living, with its provisions for transportation, housekeeping, chores and meals, to the skilled nursing home, is a leap that ignores the interim step of assisted living.

## ENTRY FEES (ENDOWMENT OR ACCOMMODATION FEES)

Historically, life-care communities charged entry fees that were all or most of a resident's total assets without provision for refund. This gradually evolved into a fixed entry fee, again without refund, and finally into a partially refundable fee that declined with length of residency. The entrance of private corporations into the field, and the competition they engendered, was the catalyst that radically changed refund practices. Now several refund policy alternatives exist—often within the same community. There are still some communities that do not have any refund policy, but these are a small handful of the older projects.

A few communities provide a 30-to-90-day adjustment period, which allows a resident to withdraw without financial penalty, but most CCRCs consider the first 10% of the entry fee as nonrefundable from the moment a resident takes occupancy of a unit. The remaining 90% (or lesser portion) of the entry fee is refunded to a resident in case of withdrawal or to her heirs in case of death in one of the following ways:

**The traditional plan.** The remaining 90% of the entry fee is reduced by 2% a month until a zero balance is reached, in 45 months. Some communities reduce the refund by 3% a month, and others deduct nursing home charges from the entry fee refund. Recent New York State legislation mandates a refund in the case of death or withdrawal of the entry fee less 2% a month, with a processing charge of not more than 4%.

**Refunds without deductions.** Many CCRCs are now offering 90% (or less) refunds without deductions. These refund plans do not decline by a certain percentage each month, but remain at 90% until the resident leaves or dies. The refund is often payable on resale of the unit or after the passage of a calendar year, whichever is first.

**A mix.** Many communities not only vary the above plans, but offer new residents a mix of these plans. It is sometimes possible to increase the entry fee in order to reduce the amount of monthly payment. There is an intention to tailor refund and entry fee plans to meet differing financial needs and capabilities.

A simple rule of thumb is that the community that returns the largest part of the entry fee with the least restrictions will require the highest entry fee.

## NONPROFIT ENTRY FEES

The American Association of Homes for the Aging in Washington, D.C., is the professional organization for nonprofit CCRCs and other health-related facilities. Its National Continuing Care Directory, revised in 1988, lists 366 life-care communities. The breakdown of refund policies for these facilities is as follows:

| | | |
|---|---|---|
| Those that do not make refunds | 26 | (7%) |
| Those refunds that decline over time | 281 | (77%) |
| Those that refund all or most of the fee | 24 | (7%) |
| Those that offer a choice of plans | 35 | (10%) |
| Total | 366 | |

## ENTRY FEES IN FOR-PROFIT COMMUNITIES

The entry of private corporations into the field is so new that there is no reliable database. However, we can generalize that virtually all for-profit life-care communities offer some type of refund plan, and the most common is the 90% refund on a 2%-a-month declining balance. It is often common for these communities to offer a choice of refund plans, with varying amounts for the entry fee. LCS, in its company-owned projects, considers 90% of the entry fee to be a loan to the corporation. It secures the indebtedness by issuing a mortgage indenture that is subordinate to other first liens, and therefore is actually a second mortgage. After death or withdrawal, it makes a full refund (of the 90%) when the unit is resold or within one year, which-ever is earlier.

## RANGE OF ENTRY FEES

It would seem logical that since life care functions as an insurance program for long-term health care, entry fees would be calibrated according to a resident's age and state of health at the time of admission. However, entry fees and monthly charges are instead based on the size of the unit occupied, with some variation for the type of refund policy selected.

Entry fees vary greatly with geographic location. For example, LCS has a project in Delray Beach, Florida, that is located directly on the Intercoastal Waterway and charges an entry fee of $400,000; in Lakewood, New Jersey, a similar unit goes for $116,000.

At the other end of the scale, The American Association of Homes for the Aging Directory lists 31 communities with entrance fees of less than $20,000. It should be pointed out that those CCRCs with extremely low entrance fees are older communities that usually only offer single rooms or studio apartments. This same directory lists one entrance fee in excess of $200,000. The majority of the nonprofit units were priced in the $40,000–$70,000 range for a one-bedroom apartment. In 1986, the national average for a nonprofit, one-bedroom unit was $58,637.

The newer communities seem oriented toward a slightly more affluent group. Listed below are the entry fees and monthly charges for a single occupancy in several new projects:

**Sample Entrance Fees for Life-Care Communities (1989)**

| Type of Apartment | Entrance Fee | Monthly Charge |
|---|---|---|
| Project A (Nonprofit): Refund declines by 2% a month | | |
| Studio | $ 65,550 | $1,060 |
| 1 bedroom | $ 88,667 | $1,280 |
| 2 bedroom | $110,939 | $1,490 |
| Project A (Nonprofit): Refund is a fixed 67% | | |
| Studio | $ 88,456 | $1,060 |
| 1 bedroom | $119,383 | $1,270 |
| 2 bedroom | $149,256 | $1,480 |
| Project B (For-profit): Refund declines by 2% a month | | |
| Studio | $ 60,500 | $ 995 |
| 1 bedroom | $ 73,400 | $1,195 |
| 2 bedroom | $ 95,600 | $1,295 |

**Sample Entrance Fees for Life-Care Communities (1989) (cont.)**

| Type of Apartment | Entrance Fee | Monthly Charge |
|---|---|---|
| Project B (For-profit): Refund is a fixed 90% | | |
| Studio | $ 80,500 | $  995 |
| 1 bedroom | $ 97,900 | $1,195 |
| 2 bedroom | $127,500 | $1,395 |
| Project C (Nonprofit): Refund is a fixed 90%, less any nursing home charges | | |
| Studio | NA | |
| 1 bedroom | $125,000 | $1,380 |
| 2 bedroom | $165,000 | $1,820 |
| Project D (For-profit): Refund is a fixed 90% | | |
| Studio | $ 85,000 | $  831 |
| 1 bedroom | $126,000 | $  900 |
| 2 bedroom | $185,000 | $1,058 |

The above projects are located in suburban areas in various Northeastern states. They all include one meal a day in their monthly fee and all-inclusive nursing home charges, with the exception of the one project that deducts the nursing home costs from any entry fee refund.

## EQUITY PARTICIPATION IN LIFE CARE

The Forum Group, through its subsidiary, Forum Life Care, Inc., began construction in 1990 of a cooperative life-care community. Located on 54 acres 45 miles south of San Francisco, The Forum at Rancho San Antonio will contain 319 units and an 81-bed nursing center.

Prices will range from $242,000 for the smallest unit, up to $595,000 for a 1,400 square foot villa. Residents will receive one meal a day and have guaranteed access to the nursing home. In the event a resident should die or leave the community, his or her share of the cooperative may be sold, although the community will retain half of any real estate appreciation on the sale.

Short nursing home stays will be paid by the residents' monthly charge, while lengthy or permanent stays will be financed through sale of the unit.

Since the community is structured as a cooperative, its board of directors is elected by the residents and control of the project rests with the shareholders.

This project has just been completed, and therefore there are no data with which to evaluate the financing. Forum Life Care has two other projects under development that will be structured on a similar basis.

This project has two revolutionary aspects: equity participation by the shareholders and the community, and resident participation on the board of directors. This industry is indeed in a state of flux.

## MONTHLY CHARGES

Two-thirds of the nonprofit life-care communities listed in the AAHA Directory had monthly charges that ran from $500 to $900 a month, with an average of $871 a month.* The increase in monthly billings for a second person occupying the units was from $300 to $500 a month.

The average monthly charge for the new projects we investigated was $1,217 a month, with an additional $542 a month for a second person.

As the project matures the monthly charges must and will increase. The manner in which this increase is determined is of prime importance to the resident. In some instances, increases are tied to the general financial health of the community. A preferable alternative found in other residency agreements is to stipulate an outside factor, such as the Consumer Price Index, as the mechanism by which increases are determined.

The American Association of Homes for the Aging reports that the average yearly increase of monthly fees by their members were as follows:

| | |
|---|---|
| 1985 | +6.2% |
| 1986 | +5.8% |
| 1987 | +4.8% |
| 1988 | +5.8% |
| 1989 | +6.1% |

## PROFIT VERSUS NONPROFIT

Surprisingly, monthly charges are usually less in a new for-profit facility than in a new nonprofit community. The private corporation is usually more liberal in its refund policies, and when this is taken into consideration, the entry fees are also less than those of nonprofit CCRCs.

Successful and mature nonprofit life-care communities (more than 10 to 12 years old) will generally have lower entry and monthly fees, but far less liberal refund policies. However, these projects have long waiting lists (one to five years).

For-profit communities will have more luxurious amenities such as indoor pools. On the other hand, none of the for-profit communities investigated had assisted-living units or the capability to deliver long-term custodial care to their residents. Half of the nonprofit communities provided these important features.

## WHAT'S THE BEST BUY?

Selecting a life-care community is not a question of obtaining the best buy, nor is the most expensive community necessarily best. An informed decision covers a matrix of financial, health and personal considerations. The management capabilities of the project's administration are also crucial in the survival of the community and in its ability to deliver care as promised.

# CHAPTER 13

# TROUBLE IN PARADISE: Life-care Problems

## Some Go Belly-up

The intricacies of life-care financing, its long-term-care features and the necessity to plan years in advance make these communities particularly vulnerable to failure through poor planning.

When a life-care community fails, it affects one of the most vulnerable portions of our population, the elderly. Community bankruptcy is doubly poignant because it destroys the financial haven that initially attracted residents to this lifestyle. It will strike while some residents are permanent occupants of the nursing home and therefore physically and emotionally unable to make radical changes in their lives. Many of the residents will have utilized a large portion of their assets to pay the entry fee, and will now face poverty.

Although the possibility of fraud always exists, most failed life-care communities are victims of mismanagement. Complex day-to-day operational problems are compounded by the necessity for advance financial and actuarial planning. It takes more than a decade for the new community to mature and failure to anticipate this changing future will destroy the community's financial integrity.

The corporation, whether for-profit or nonprofit, must plan for the ordinary depreciation of the physical plant and also for a radical shift in the financial resources of the nursing home. When a project first opens its doors, the nursing home is profitable because it accepts private patients from outside the community. Later, this situation reverses and forces the nursing home into deficit financing as more and more of its own residents occupy its beds.

The properly managed community will maintain reserve funds for future health needs. It must also keep generous funds in reserve for maintaining the property. Life care is essentially risk pooling. In order for this concept to work, residents who die must be replaced by new residents. Therefore, the project must be maintained in pristine condition to attract the necessary new prospects. Failure to fill vacancies reduces the size of the risk pool and places everyone at risk.

Residents must realize that they do not have good legal protection for their entry fee. Residents do not have a recordable real estate interest. A life-care contract is an occupancy license that runs to the corporation. In the event of the community's bankruptcy, the resident is usually only one in a long line of unsecured creditors. The community's real estate will be encumbered with mortgage loans that take precedence over all other creditors. As the project stumbles into financial difficulties, creditors who provide goods and services will be the first to become aware of cash shortages and will promptly file their liens. The residents will be the last to know of the problems, and their claims will be so far behind others that any chance of recovery will be negligible.

An exception to this was discovered in the practices of one large developer. This corporation treats 90% of the entry fee as a loan and files a mortgage lien on the property on behalf of the resident. The terms of this indenture make it secondary to the corporation's primary borrowings, so in effect it is a second mortgage, making it more likely (but not guaranteeing) that the resident will receive at least a partial refund.

Dr. H. S. Ruchlin in a 1988 article entitled "Continuing Care Retirement Communities: An Analysis of Financial Viability and Health Care Coverage," in the *Gerontologist*, reported that one-third of all CCRCs have a negative net income or negative net worth. Other authorities explain that all CCRCs will have negative income at times, but that reserves or interest on reserves should be sufficient to pay these deficits. A negative net worth would have more serious consequences.

In those states that have legislation regulating life care, the project sales personnel will tell prospective residents that their interests are well protected by the laws, and they need not worry. This is not necessarily the case!

# HORROR STORIES

## NEW CONSTRUCTION

In its February 1990 issue, *Consumer Reports* tells the story of Notchcliff in northern Maryland. This community, placed in a country setting not far from Baltimore, was planned for 114 cluster homes built near a core of 101 apartments. However, only 15 of the 114 cluster homes were sold and occupied. Since the sponsors had counted on entry fee income to carry the debt load, they were unable to continue. In mid-1988 this project went into bankruptcy. Court-appointed trustees hired a management concern to run Notchcliff, but were unable to arrange a sale of the project. Seventy residents still remain and are subject to foreclosure and complete loss of any investment they made in the community.

A failure to sell units can be a financial problem for any construction project, including condominiums, cooperatives or single-home tract developments. However, conventional real estate developments have alternatives available to them—they can rent units, instead of selling them, cut back on the scope of construction or lower sales prices. Life-care communities, because of their unique structure and risk-pooling feature, find it difficult to implement these options. For this reason, many states that regulate life care require that half of the units be sold before construction commences.

## A MATURE COMMUNITY—PACIFIC HOMES

In 1912, the German Methodist Conference of California established a home for retired ministers at one of its campgrounds. In 1929, the Conference merged with the Methodist Episcopal Church and incorporated the Pacific Old People's Home as a nonprofit corporation. From 1949 to 1964 six additional properties were assembled and incorporated under the name of Pacific Homes Corporation. These were life-care communities as we know them; they had entry fees, monthly charges and guaranteed health care. The community operated under the regulations of the State of California, which was one of the first states to pass laws concerning life care.

When this well-established, church-affiliated group of communities began to have financial problems, the State Department of Social Welfare was notified. This department postponed filing priority liens on behalf of the residents as it was able to do under the regulations, in order to give the corporation an opportunity to obtain new financing for reorganization. When the complete structure finally collapsed and the liens were filed, they were at the end of a long line of prior encumbrances. Moreover, although the ability to file priority liens did not help Pacific Home residents, even this protection is not presently available because of changes in the federal bankruptcy laws.

The age of this community, its church affiliation and the state regulations would seem to have been sufficient to safeguard the residents. However, as the report on the feasibility of the trustees' plan to reorganize Pacific Homes states, "One of the key ingredients to long-term viability is adequate cash reserves." The report went on to recommend ". . . operational reserves to cover normal operating expenses due to unforeseen drops in occupancy, slow pay, or other unforeseen expenses, equal to 30 to 45 days of cash operating expenses [and] . . . future liability reserves of 6 months operating expenses for the future replacement of property, plant and equipment, and to protect against future expenses and liabilities.''

## SALES REPRESENTATIONS

It is important to remember that a new life-care community, whether non-profit or for-profit, will hire a professional marketing team to sell its units. A good proportion of the 10% of the entry fee considered earned income at the time of resident occupancy will go toward sales efforts.

The salesperson will usually have a real estate background and work on commission. He or she will go by various names such as Adult Counselor, Moving Specialist, Life-Care Coordinator or Unit Designer.

Sales efforts are primarily directed toward apartment appearance, available amenities, with health and physical security. Any representations made by marketing personnel are not binding unless they are a part of the occupancy agreement. If a matter is interpretive, an officer of the corporation should be the one to clarify the matter, in written form.

Either through direction or misdirection, sales personnel often make sweeping generalizations such as, ''The state regulations protect your investment,'' or, ''Our skilled nursing home will be sufficient for any health requirements.''

Without the trained advice of a real estate attorney and a tax consultant, many prospective residents erroneously believe that they are purchasing a condominium.

## GOVERNMENT REGULATIONS

At present only 22 states have any legislation regulating these communities (see appendix for a full list of those states). In states without any legislation, lawsuits have been brought for certain disputes, especially concerning contract terminations and refunds. In general, suits brought by residents themselves have been successful, while those brought by heirs of residents have not.

Until 1989, New York State had laws that prohibited the prepayment of nursing home charges for more than three months. These laws existed to keep nursing homes from demanding huge entrance deposits in exchange for waiting list placement. This protection also made it impossible for life-care communities to operate in that state. Specific legislation signed by the governor in 1989 now allows for life care.

The federal government does not regulate these facilities in any manner unless their nursing homes are Medicare/Medicaid approved. In that instance the nursing home facilities would have to abide by the applicable federal-state regulations. There are some technical IRS rulings concerning these projects. One provision pertains to imputed interest if the entry fee is treated by the sponsor as a loan. Another concerns that portion of the entry fee or monthly charges that can be considered health insurance. These are technical tax questions that should be thoroughly discussed with the prospective resident's tax adviser.

As was stated earlier, even if the community's nursing home is not Medicare/Medicaid approved, this part of the facility will still fall under the applicable state regulations that affect all nursing homes.

The 22 regulated states do not provide the resident protection to the extent salespeople may lead you to believe. In many instances, the overseeing agency (which can be any state agency from the Department of Insurance or Aging, to the Department of Health) has few regulatory powers. Its mission in overseeing life care is primarily to monitor these communities and provide consumer protection information for resident applicants. In the event a monitoring agency discovers a problem, it must refer the matter to the state's attorney general for prosecution. This sequence could take months, far too long to avert financial mismanagement.

Even in those states where the responsible agency does have enforcement powers, the regulations are far from extensive.

## A SUMMARY OF STATE LAWS

**Most regulated states require**

Complete financial disclosure to the applicant

Escrow for down payments

Refunds for those who change their mind before occupancy

That certain provisions be contained in the contract

Firm deposits on half the units before construction begins

**Only half the regulated states require**

Regulatory power in the supervising state agency

Any reserves at all

Actuarial studies

For those states that require reserves, they usually equal one month's operating expenses and one year's debt payment and interest.

## RESERVES

The reserve requirements listed above are similar to the recommendations suggested by the trustees in the bankruptcy of Pacific Homes. Yet one month's operating expenses hardly seems adequate, since if a community were to be in dire financial shape, it would have exhausted its credit far beyond one month's goods and services.

Some communities have been known to utilize two distinct corporations, with one company operating the community while a second holds the assets. If the resident contracts run to the corporation with zero assets, there is absolutely no financial protection.

New York State had the benefit of the other states' experience when it came time for it to draft its laws. As a consequence, many of its provisions are stricter than those found in other states. For example, New York requires mandatory reserves equal to principal, interest, taxes and insurance for 12 months, repairs and replacement costs for 12, and operating cost reserves for six months.

They also give the State Superintendent of Insurance the authority to dictate reserve levels.

## FINANCIAL STATEMENTS

Since a resident's entry fee is not legally well protected, there is a cardinal rule that should be observed concerning life-care community financial statements: **Do not deal with any community that will not willingly provide full financial information.**

If a community is mature it has a financial track record that can be evaluated by your CPA. Evaluating a new project is a bit more difficult. The states that have disclosure laws usually require the disclosure of the current balance sheet and operating statement, and financial projections for the next five years. Since no uniform accounting procedures exist for the industry, and future projections can be arrived at by a number of methods, determining the true financial feasibility of the project can be nearly impossible. With enough information, your CPA may be able to tell whether proper reserves have been established, whether the permanent financing is reasonable, and whether the community is on financially sound footing.

## WHY DO THEY FAIL?

An understanding of why some communities fail might allow the consumer to better evaluate life-care management.

## MISMANAGEMENT

This is a sin that can be found in the management of any enterprise, from the smallest convenience store to the largest manufacturing company. The problem is sometimes compounded in life care when individuals entering the field from backgrounds in church organizations or social work lack the necessary management skills. For this reason, many nonprofit sponsors have elected to hire professional management groups to run their projects.

Mismanagement in life care is not by any means restricted to nonprofit communities. Private real estate developers, accustomed to finishing one project and moving on to another, may be blind to the long-term requirements of a life-care community.

## INADEQUATE CAPITALIZATION AND RESERVES

The lack of proper start-up capital is a problem for communities in their early stages. The failure to establish, maintain and replenish cash reserves is disastrous. If any one element were to be singled out for the failure of these communities, it would be inadequate cash reserves to cover physical maintenance, increased health-care costs, economic downturns and other contingencies.

## FRAUD

In its initial phases, a life-care community will generate a great deal of money, enough to provide a strong temptation for the unscrupulous, who might try to siphon the money from a project and disappear before their malfeasance was discovered.

## ACTUARIAL VARIATION

This is an area of potential difficulty caused by random deviation from what was assumed to be the statistical norms. It may not be the fault of planners, but prudence dictates that reserves be allocated conservatively in order to compensate for this possibility.

The actuarial data compiled by the insurance industry are based on the general population and are not geared to the 200 or 300 residents of a single community. While death rates or nursing home occupancy rates can be predicted accurately for a large population, a single community might temporarily experience a significant shift above or below those norms.

Oddly enough, even excessive good health can harm a community, as it could throw actuarial planning out of kilter. Conversely, if a community experienced a higher-than-expected demand for nursing home beds, it might not be able to accommodate all its residents in the facility and would have to contract with outside nursing homes for additional space. Either circumstance, if persisting long enough, would affect expenses and reserves.

The American Association of Homes for the Aging is attempting to establish a database for life-care communities. This effort is still in its early stages. At present, planners must work with inadequate data.

# CHAPTER 14

# HOW TO CHOOSE A LIFE-CARE COMMUNITY: Ten Steps

## Take Your Time

We have profiled life-care communities and indicated their important place in the elderly housing continuum. A series of pitfalls have been presented that are serious enough to make prudent investors wary. We recommend that your decision-making process incorporate the following 10 steps. Some of the warnings and suggestions have been previously mentioned before, but their importance requires repetition.

## The Steps

### STEP ONE: DECIDE IF YOU REALLY WANT TO LIVE THERE.

After you have checked out the physical amenities of the community, fire safety and elderly adaptations, you must decide if you really want to live there. Congregate living is not for everyone. You will become part of a small village where resident councils and management will create a great many rules you will have to live by.

If the project is currently in operation, make arrangements to spend a night or two as a visitor. This will allow you to sample meals, observe your future neighbors first hand and get a true feeling about the community's atmosphere.

## STEP TWO: FIND OUT YOUR STATE LAWS.

Contact your state's Department of Aging (or its equivalent) to get any information it may have concerning the communities in your area. If your state has regulating legislation, this Agency will inform you which office within the state government has the prime responsibility for life care.

If the responsible agency does not have a brochure or other material concerning your state's legislation, get the statute numbers from it. Almost all town libraries have a copy of the state statutes, and when you know the law numbers, the appropriate sections are not difficult to locate.

## STEP THREE: LOOK FOR AAHA ACCREDITATION.

This is not a necessity, but it would be a helpful safeguard. The Continuing Care Accreditation Commission is an independent group sponsored by the American Association of Homes for the Aging (AAHA). AAHA is a professional organization composed of more than 3,000 nonprofit nursing homes, custodial facilities and life-care communities. The 14-member commission, aided by an advisory financial panel, is composed of experts in the life-care field. They investigate and review findings for communities that apply for accreditation, which for-profit and nonprofit communities may do after they have been in operation for one year and have an occupancy rate of 90%.

The commission reviews financial statements and life-care contracts and inspects the premises for maintenance, health and safety standards. They evaluate whether the residents' physical needs are met and also their quality of life. Investigators spend three days at a community and additional time reviewing all necessary files and documents.

As of 1990, 91 communities in 20 states had been accredited, with a 10% failure rate by others. Some communities are granted conditional accreditation with the understanding that they will correct certain deficiencies. The primary reason that some CCRCs fail is lack of proper reserves for future health-care commitments.

We do not make this accreditation a definite requirement in the selection process for several reasons: Many new communities do not qualify for consideration under the one-year rule; the community must pay for the investigation, and this is expensive; for-profit communities may apply, but so far virtually all those that have applied are nonprofit facilities.

## STEP FOUR: CHECK THE BOOKS.

Chapter Eleven emphasized the point that you should not deal with any community that will not willingly provide financial information. Failure to comply with this rule is the equivalent of purchasing a house without checking the title.

If your state has disclosure laws, this information will be available to you. If the project is constructed under the ownership of a very large corporation, remember that, while the consolidated financial statement of the parent company might be extremely solid, it could sell the community at some future date to a less reliable group.

If you are considering entering a mature community, have your bank request a credit report on the operation. If they are listed as "slow pay" or have liens or judgments against them—beware!

## STEP FIVE: CHECK ON PEOPLE.

Benevolent sponsors can be honest but naive. Sincerity does not mean that they know how to run a food service program. The business and life-care background of sponsors, management and staff is of incalculable importance to the success of the community.

Speak with several present residents. Are they happy with the services and the attitude and cooperation of the management? They may know things you would rather not discover for yourself.

Observe, as far as you can, the health of recently admitted residents. In order for life care to work, residents should be in moderately good health at the time of admission. If new residents seem overly frail or infirm, the community has lowered its health admission standards, which may indicate a problem with a low occupancy rate. Accepting any prospect who arrives with entry fee in hand may help solve the present financial crunch, but it can jeopardize the whole concept of risk-pooling health care.

## STEP SIX: CHECK OUT THE NURSING HOME AS IF YOU ARE GOING TO ENTER IT TOMORROW.

For you may. When you enter a life-care community you have chosen your future nursing home. Make sure that this is the facility you prefer. Community administrators say that many prospective residents do not even enter the nursing home. If the facility is part of the tour, they seem uncomfortable, ask few questions and can't wait to continue on to the next stop on their itinerary.

Inspection standards and most state regulations require nursing homes to provide their last two inspection reports to the public. Report deficiencies may be of an inconsequential nature, but are serious if they indicate poor nursing care, excessive bed sores or misuse of chemical and physical restraints.

If the community is new, or still under construction, a physical inspection of the nursing home may not be possible. Conversations can still be held with the medical director and administrator. They should be asked about their attitudes concerning such important items as

- **the use of physical and chemical restraints.** The misuse of restraints, and by that we mean overuse, is one of the most common faults of nursing homes. While a simple waist restraint for the stroke patient with poor balance is acceptable, restraining a confused patient to a wheelchair is not. A continent and ambulatory patient who is physically restrained will shortly become incontinent and nonambulatory. Physical restraints in nursing homes are often used by harried or overworked staff members who do not wish to deal properly with confused patients. Since many elderly with senile dementia tend to lose track of time, nursing home personnel will often use chemical restraints to calm them. The nursing home management should have a consistent and reasonable policy on the use of restraints.
- **bed sores.** Bed sores are preventable, but if they occur can be difficult or sometimes impossible to cure. They most often occur with the bedridden incontinent patient who is not turned often enough. The administration should have a firm policy on this matter.
- **senile dementia** (most often Alzheimer's disease). Some Alzheimer's patients will become combative and filled with a compulsive wanderlust during the midphase of their affliction. Properly trained nursing personnel will know how to handle these patients, calm them and keep them from harm. The administration's philosophy about this situation is of particular importance to the life-care resident because of the termination clauses in the occupancy agreement. Almost all such agreements have a paragraph that allows for termination if the resident is a danger to herself or others. A ''sundowning'' Alzheimer's patient (one who tends to turn night into day), can indeed wander from a facility and come into harm's way.

  Such a patient will often enter other patients' rooms and be generally disruptive both physically and verbally. These situations can be controlled by the properly trained and compassionate staff, but they are time-consuming and fraught with problems.
- **their philosophy on activities of daily living.** It is often more efficient for the staff to aid a patient with these routine self-care functions. It is far easier to brush a stroke patient's hair than stand by while she struggles to perform this now difficult task for herself. However, proper nursing requires that patients be encouraged to perform all reasonably possible ADLs.

For further information on how to evaluate and choose a nursing home, we refer you to *Nursing Home: The Complete Guide,* by the same authors (Facts on File, 1990).

As the community matures, nursing home beds should be available for approximately 17% of the community. Find out which outside nursing home would be utilized if no vacancies existed at the time that space was needed. How many beds do they keep open at any given time for residents?

## STEP SEVEN: EXPLORE THE ARRANGEMENTS FOR ASSISTED LIVING.

Although the need for this type of care may occur suddenly, in most instances people who are able to live independently one day do not go to a skilled nursing home the next. Yet more than half of all life-care communities omit the crucial midstep between independent living and the nursing home. Residents who need assisted living require part-time help on a daily basis. They probably do not need nursing care but might require help in dressing, transferring (moving from bed to chair to toilet, etc.), bathing, or any other activities of daily living. If they are "forgetful," they might require protective oversight and the dispensing of medications. These individuals do not need the labor-intensive nursing care that a nursing home provides. Economically, it is wasteful to consign semi-independent people to a nursing home. Emotionally, it can be disastrous.

Life-care sales personnel often do not point out the alternative of assisted living, simply because they do not provide it. The proper questions are not asked by prospective residents because they tend to view nursing homes in the broadest possible sense—"a nursing home is where you go when you can't make it in your apartment." If the life-care concept is truly viable and it is to have its proper place in the elderly housing continuum, two aspects of assisted living must be present. First, part-time help should be available to the resident if she is able to remain in her apartment. Second, special assisted-living units, near the nursing home, should be available for those who cannot live independently but who do not need to enter the skilled nursing home.

Home care is often available on a fee-for-service basis from outside providers, and some for-profit communities have gone so far as to form their own home-care agencies, whose fees are not covered under the life-care contract. However, several problems are associated with attempting to arrange home care with outside agencies:

It is expensive. The House Committee on Aging estimates that payment for a home health aide runs from $11 to $20 per hour, depending on the geographic location. Even minimum help of 15 hours a week is beyond the budget of many.

Individuals suffering the early stages of senile dementia might tend to wander, perform dangerous activities and need more oversight than an hour or two a day would provide, yet still not need to enter a skilled nursing home.

In certain areas, reliable home health care agencies are not available, or those that do exist cannot supply trustworthy and competent individuals.

Pennswood Village, a nonprofit continuing care retirement village located 25 miles from Philadelphia, solves this problem by providing two nursing facilities. With a total of 375 residents, this community also runs Woolman House, a skilled nursing facility with 45 beds. It also has Barclay House, a personal care facility, with 41 private rooms.

Private developers constructing a new community know that their skilled nursing home will be profitable immediately and continue to be so until residents occupy the majority of the beds. A personal care (or assisted-living) facility would not generate profit and would only use up construction dollars without any present or future return. This void will become more obvious as these communities mature. It is possible to control the census in a skilled nursing home to a certain extent. With the new DRG rules, acute care hospitals discharge terminal patients, many of which transfer to nursing homes until death. A nursing home, which wished a certain number of vacant beds, say a year from now, could plan their admissions accordingly. It might stay away from the chronic patient with an indefinite prognosis. This means that upon opening, a CCRC can fill up most of its nursing home beds with lucrative private pay patients, and then gradually change its mix as bed use for its residents is anticipated.

The whole actuarial base of a CCRC requires the admission of residents who are basically in good health at the time of admission. This means that assisted-living units must remain mostly vacant until they are gradually filled by residents. They cannot be utilized by any sizable number of outsiders since their very definition requires chronic conditions or an indefinite stay. Private developers just skip over it and state that a nursing home is a nursing home—which it isn't.

## STEP EIGHT: DON'T INSIST ON "THE BEST BARGAIN."

Life-care financial structuring is such that cheaper is not necessarily better. Assuming that amenities, health care and refund policies were equal, price comparisons would be in order. However, beware of communities that:

**Offer a discount.** They may have a high vacancy rate; this is a problem unto itself, and there may be underlying reasons for this that are not readily apparent.

**Offer to freeze monthly charges.** This is an economic impossibility and will only jeopardize the community's future.

**Are using entry fees to fund present costs.** A careful review of all the financial documents should reveal if this is taking place.

**Tell you that they are fully backed by the financial resources of XYZ Church.** They aren't telling the truth. What other falsehoods are they telling?

**Tell you not to worry about little details missing from the contract.** If it's not there, you probably won't get it.

**Tell you not to waste money having your lawyer and accountant check documentation.** What are they worried about?

**Tell you that their financial information is confidential.** Keep looking.

### STEP NINE: HAVE YOUR ACCOUNTANT AND LAWYER GO OVER ALL DOCUMENTATION AND FINANCIAL STATEMENTS.

### STEP TEN: THE CONTRACT IS THE BIBLE. USE THE FOLLOWING CHECKLIST FOR A SURVEY OF ITS COMPLETENESS:

## CHARGES AND FEES

Preoccupancy or deposit agreements. These should not exceed more than 10% of the entry fee and should be held in an escrow account. There must be provision for refund in the event of death or cancellation. Cancellation procedures should be spelled out.

Entry-fee refunds. The contract should clearly identify the reasons for entry-fee refunds (death or departure), the time frame of payment, amount and any charges or fees that may be deducted.

Monthly charges. The amount of present monthly charges for single or double occupancy must be listed, along with the frequency with which they can be raised. It is preferred that increases be indexed to an objective factor such as the Consumer Price Index. Temporary or permanent residence in the nursing home may require fee adjustments. The exact method of computing these changes should be part of the contract.

Miscellaneous fees. You do not want to find a monthly surprise package in your mailbox. If there are to be any additional charges, for any reason other than services you purchase, they should be enumerated. Outside provider expenses such as telephone bills, TV cable service and beauty parlors are to be expected. One corporation adds a $50-a-month management fee to the charges. It is just such an item that might initially go unnoticed. The payment by the community of all utility charges except the telephone must be reflected in the contract.

Nonpayment penalties. Adverse circumstances or temporary cash flow problems can affect anyone. The community's procedure for treating this problem, and more devastating financial reversals, should be a matter of record.

## THE APARTMENT UNIT

Identification. The unit's exact location and description should be given.

Extra space. It is customary to provide residential storage space in the building's basement and parking for one vehicle in a space near the unit.

Housekeeping. If this service is provided, and it often is, the contract should specify how often the apartment is cleaned. Heavy work such as windows and carpet cleaning will be done periodically, at the intervals specified.

Routine maintenance. This should include necessary carpentry, electrical work and plumbing at no cost to the resident.

Linens. Many communities provide bed and bath linens to the residents on a weekly basis, at no additional charge.

Laundry. Personal laundry is done by the resident in a conveniently located laundry center. The proximity of this center to the unit is important.

Guests. Overnight guests cannot be precluded, although time restrictions on young visitors may prevail. Provisions for remarriage should be specified.

Pets. Animals are usually allowed, but there may be restrictions on their size and behavior.

Appliances. The type of kitchen and other appliances and their maintenance and replacement schedule should be spelled out.

Emergency call system. The presence of the call system in each unit and the medical center's method of response should be indicated in the contract.

## HEALTH CARE

Nursing home costs. If the nursing home costs are all-inclusive within the terms of the contract, it should be so stated. The exact terms of modified nursing home coverage must be explicitly covered. If there are any other costs for nursing home patients, such as for additional meals, they must be enumerated.

Assisted living. The contract will indicate the availability of any assisted-living units or home health care services available. The terms and conditions of this care are an integral part of the agreement.

The determination of nursing home entry. This important decision cannot be left to the administrator or the medical director. It should be made in consultation with the resident's personal physician.

Outside nursing homes. If all nursing home expenses are covered under an all-inclusive contract, and beds are not available, it must be stated in the contract that the community will make arrangements and pay for temporary care in a specifically designated outside facility.

Retention of the resident's apartment. A resident may have an indeterminate stay in an acute-care hospital or the community nursing home. If so, it is important to know how long the living unit may be retained before reoccupancy.

Insurance required. Life care usually requires Medicare Parts A and B along with a Medigap policy. The management must indicate exactly what benefits are required in this ancillary insurance.

## TERMINATION

The circumstances under which the community can terminate the contract.

The circumstances under which the resident may terminate the contract and get back the refund.

The rights of a surviving spouse.

## MEALS

The number and type of meals included in the contract

Availability of apartment tray service on medical advice

Provisions for special diets (such as vegetarian or kosher)

Meal availability and cost for guests

## ADDITIONAL SERVICES

The type, frequency and destination of free transportation

Security provisions

Recreational activities offered

Grounds maintenance

Use of common areas

The right to form a residents' council.

*Note:* Some minor items, pet regulations as an example, may be included in the resident's handbook. All prospective residents should read this material to see whether they are in agreement with its general philosophy. These rules should be a joint effort of the administration and the residents' council.

# LIFE CARE SUMMARIZED

## THE CONCEPT

The attributes of life care and the satisfaction of several emotional and physical needs that membership in one of these communities gives seem to overwhelm criticism. These elderly havens are not only a positive step in the housing continuum but actually contain several stages of senior housing needs.

For the aging elderly who have spent their more active years in travel, Sun Belt activity or merely staying on in their own homes, this housing alternative provides several answers. For the still-active, it provides smaller and more manageable living accommodations with chore service, transportation and meals if and when desired. The premises are elder friendly and the congregate services can be utilized if and when frailty increases. Chronic physical and/or mental infirmities may require transfer to the assisted-living units or the project's skilled nursing home. Since these are moves within the neighborhood, they are accomplished with far less mental anguish than faced by the general population.

This lifestyle also maintains financial independence, which is important to many. Payment of an entry fee and capped monthly charges guarantees care without the onerous "spend down" provisions of Medicaid entitlement. Families are not burdened with the physical and emotional problems of elder care, while a new movement in the field allows for large returns of the entry fee to the resident's estate.

As the elderly approach their mid-seventies and become concerned about future health and self-maintenance, life care is an alternative that should be seriously explored.

## COSTS AND PLANS

One of the important benefits of these communities is the freedom from financial and physical worry. Entering a plan that did not include an all-inclusive (completely prepaid) nursing home destroys that benefit. Consideration of other plans such as fee-for-service or partial pay destroys an attractive concept of life care and may place the resident in future financial jeopardy. An analysis of the newer communities reveals that those that are rationally financed can provide this service to their residents within affordable parameters.

Monthly charges must be capped and hopefully indexed to annual increases of the Consumer Price Index. The amount of this fee should be less than the rate charged by area senior congregate housing that provides comparable services (excluding health care).

A minimum of 90% of the entry fee must be refundable in the event of death or a move. Astute for-profit sponsors of these projects are well aware of the time value of money, and many are now providing full 90% refunds. However, so many of the projects are tied to the "traditional" refund plan of 90% less a declining balance of 2% a month, that this plan may have to be considered. There is another exception to refunds as they pertain to mature nonprofit communities. In this instance, the entry fund requirements will be so far below newer construction that the competitive edge will be apparent. Unfortunately, these communities will have the longest waiting lists.

## You're Ready to Go

Remember, you are more likely to require assisted living than you are a nursing home, and yet only one-third of these communities include this option in their plan.

Life-care living is congregate living, and the largest complaint about that alternative was the lack of a full kitchen in some projects.

Many of the projects are constructed with garden-style buildings interconnected with a core building that contains the dining room, nursing home and other amenities. It is recommended that an apartment unit be obtained as near to this core as possible.

## The Final Word

It is the physical, health and financial security that makes these communities so attractive. It is the financial underwriting of these needs a decade or two into the future that proves so difficult for managers. Improper reserve accounts are the single leading sponsor fault. We cannot think of any instance in senior housing alternatives that more certainly requires the advice of a good real estate attorney and certified public accountant than life care.

---------- PART THREE ----------

# DEPENDENT
# LIVING

The primary demarcation between assisted and dependent living for the elderly is best summed up in the phrase "protective oversight." In some of its forms, assisted living may provide all the day-to-day necessities, including congregate meals, barrier-free apartments, housekeeping and the availability of emergency medical help. If, in addition to these, an individual's activities are monitored on a continuing basis, then there is protective oversight.

Once again, individuals have a wide range of options within dependent living. These accommodations range from those for fully mobile people who need custodial or board-and-care services, to those for people with such severe disabilities that they require 24-hour-a-day skilled nursing care.

# CHAPTER 15

# BOARD AND CARE:
# Custodial Care

## A HOUSE OF MANY NAMES

A 1989 report from the House of Representatives Committee on Aging estimated that there are over 1 million elderly and disabled Americans living in 68,000 residential board-and-care facilitiés.

This type of housing is known by various names throughout the country, and often by several names within the same state. Board-and-care establishments are sometimes referred to as rest homes, retirement centers, homes for adults, personal care facilities, residential care facilities, enriched housing, domiciliary homes, assisted-living homes, class C and D boarding homes, adult group homes, homes for the aged, California community care facilities, foster care homes, shelter care homes and private proprietary homes for adults. In Canada they are usually called rest homes. Many professionals in the field prefer the term personal care facilities. Their professional organization is known as the National Association of Residential Care Facilities.

To further complicate the matter, the National Nursing Home Survey lists these institutions as residential facilities, while many professionals in the health-care field call them custodial homes. Institutions involved in custodial care may be board-and-care homes or may fall under the old definition of intermediate-care nursing homes, which did have licensed personnel and provided some nursing care.

The Select Committee on Aging for the House of Representatives defined board and care as "the broad term used to describe facilities that provide shelter, food, and protection to frail and disabled individuals."

The Denver Research Institute, which performed a study of 205 board-and-care facilities housing only the elderly for the U.S. Department of Health and Human Services, defined them as "a non-Medicaid-certified facility, licensed or unlicensed, which provides room and board, personal care, and protective oversight on a 24-hour basis for four or more adults."

## MIXED AND CONGREGATE FACILITIES

Although elderly congregate housing provides room and board along with housekeeping services, it does not offer protective oversight on a round-the-clock basis. Part-time nursing may be available at a congregate complex, and it may advertise this service. In practice, nursing care in these facilities is arranged by the administration on a fee-for-service basis. This type of care anticipates temporary help for an hour or two a day.

Large mixed-level nursing homes often have buildings or sections that provide custodial care that would somewhat qualify under our definition of board and care. The Hebrew Home for the Aged in Riverdale, New York, is an example of this type of mixed facility. This large complex is located on a site overlooking the Hudson River with a view of the New Jersey Palisades. Its 19 acres hold seven buildings that house 784 beds, including a skilled nursing home, a special Alzheimer's unit and lower levels of care, some of which are custodial in nature.

These large mixed-level institutions are primarily nursing homes, are regulated by the state as such and have licensed nursing personnel at all levels of care. These factors affect the laws under which they operate and the amount and type of care they can deliver, and therefore differentiate them from the smaller board-and-care homes.

Resident monitoring, or protective oversight, differentiates board and care from a boarding house or from a residential hotel that caters to the elderly. Homes that have only one or two residents are usually referred to as foster homes.

One board-and-care administrator summed up his facility's function as "to provide a protected environment which included three meals a day, the proper use of medications, and oversight over personal hygiene and socialization."

# A GOOD CHOICE

## DANNY T., 74

It was obvious to everyone who knew him that Danny never really recovered from his wife's death. After Mollie died three years ago, he seemed to lose all interest in life. He never called any of their friends that were still left in the neighborhood, and he spent his days slouched in his old leather chair watching television game shows.

Danny's son, Tim, lived in California, but he faithfully made two trips a year to see his father. He begged Danny to move west and live either with him or at least nearby. The suggestion was received in stony silence.

On his last trip east, Tim became very concerned about his father's condition. He found prescription drugs in the medicine chest with dates that did not correspond with the number of pills remaining. It was obvious that his father was taking his medications erratically. He also discovered that there was little food in the house. This combination might explain why his father seemed to be losing weight, was lethargic, ill-kempt and depressed.

Tim made an appointment to see the family doctor. He was told that his father never kept his last scheduled appointment and had failed to make a new one. The doctor said that in his opinion, Danny's present condition would only worsen. The depression might increase, and he would probably end up suffering from malnutrition. He was also a strong candidate for potential substance abuse. These dangers were in addition to the serious problems that might arise through Danny's failure to follow the drug regimen.

That night Tim and his father argued. Danny was intractable. The discussion turned into a shouting match. "I will not move in with my kids! I refuse to be a burden on anyone!" Danny yelled.

"Then you're going to get yourself in big trouble," his son replied.

"So, I die in my home like I'm supposed to. And maybe it's about time."

Discouraged and depressed, Tim telephoned the doctor on the following day. "I know he can't continue living alone," he said. "Maybe a nursing home is the answer?"

"Your dad doesn't need a nursing home," the doctor replied. "He's not confused, ill or incontinent. I think a board-and-care place may be the answer. I have some names for you . . ."

Tim and Danny drove slowly by the Wessex Rest Home. It was located in a part of town that had once housed wealthy merchants and their families. Most of these older large homes had been divided into small apartments. The Wessex building still retained its broad front porch, complete with rockers, although a modern wing housing the dining room and recreation hall had been added. The building had a solid and comforting aura that spoke of another age.

Wessex housed 30 older men and women. Although some residents were in wheelchairs and others used canes or walkers, everyone was able to self-transfer and were mostly continent. The administrator admitted that his staff was not medically licensed, and therefore each guest had to take his own medication. The staff would monitor time and amount. The drugs would be kept at a central work station, and at the appropriate time they would be made available to the resident. A staff member would make sure that each resident took the proper amount of medication and would reorder from the pharmacy when necessary.

The home provided three meals a day, housekeeping, laundry and transportation when necessary. A member of the staff was present around the clock to help residents with a host of tasks ranging from addressing envelopes to buttoning shirt cuffs. Rooms were shared by two people, but were personalized with each resident's belongings and furnishings. The living room was large and comfortable, with a color television in one corner and large-print books in another. The dining room held tables for four, and the recreation room housed a pool table, ceramics kiln and card tables. The building's atmosphere felt more like an old-fashioned resort hotel than a custodial nursing home.

Danny seemed pleased with the arrangements, but refused to give in easily. "Can't afford it," he snapped.

But he could. Danny's Social Security benefits in addition to his small pension check were sufficient to pay the monthly charges and leave him a small personal allowance.

On his next visit east, Tim found his father engrossed in his daily card game with new friends. Danny's physical appearance had improved, he took the proper medications daily and, more important, he seemed content.

## ANALYSIS

Tim was right to be concerned about his father's initial condition. Danny was exhibiting several behavioral patterns that often afflict members of the independent elderly. He was depressed, socially isolated, and not eating properly or following his drug regimen. Danny's problems were exacerbated by his deep depression, which is a common symptom in elderly widowers. If this mood continued, it could lead to confusion, substance abuse or suicide.

In addition to Danny's problems, some elderly tend to over-medicate. They obtain prescription drugs from several physicians, each unaware of the other. The independent advanced elderly are also susceptible to falls and other home accidents. Certain chronic medical conditions, while not acute enough for nursing home placement, might make independent living difficult. Arthritis might cause difficulty with routine household chores and certain personal care functions but still not be completely incapacitating.

Danny, like so many of the elderly, can still live a relatively independent life with some help. A board-and-care facility, which provides for his daily needs with a minimum of protective oversight, is the correct care choice.

Fortunately, the cost of these facilities is within the reach of almost everyone.

# BENEFITS OF BOARD AND CARE

These facilities have five advantages:

1.  They reduce the number of nursing home placements. Placing an ambulatory person without a debilitating chronic medical problem into a

nursing home can be emotionally devastating. In addition, it subtracts a skilled nursing home bed from the short supply. Board-and-care residents are semidependent, but they have some independence, which institutionalization would strip them of and also increase feelings of abandonment.

2. They don't feel like institutions. Nursing homes are constructed in a manner similar to acute-care hospital medical models. Residents who do not need this level of care feel "warehoused," with a resulting increase in depression. Most facilities are quite small, which gives them a home-like atmosphere not found in a larger, more complex structure.

3. They are community oriented. Because of their smaller size, board-and-care residences are apt to be housed in converted homes located in established residential areas. This places them near public transportation, churches, shopping, senior citizen centers and often the old neighborhoods of the residents. Nursing homes with mixed levels of care that include custodial are large complexes often constructed in suburban areas. This isolation reduces the residents' opportunities for outside experiences.

4. Residents can be independent. Although all residents are monitored, there is a great deal of freedom for those who are able to exercise it. Residents are encouraged to leave the premises for outings, shopping, church or just a walk in the neighborhood. Supervision in the well-run board-and-care home is circumspect. Residents go about their daily lives without feeling watched or a part of a hospital-like routine. Everyone wears his or her own clothing. Living and dining rooms, along with recreation areas, are apt to appear home-like.

5. They are affordable. The average national cost of a semi-private room in a nursing home is close to $100 a day. This sum can be far higher in certain metropolitan areas. Although there are expensive board-and-care homes, as a general rule their cost is half that of the daily rate for a skilled nursing home. Their cost can often be paid from Social Security benefits.

# WHO ARE THE RESIDENTS?

Because of licensing laws, the lack of medical personnel and the physical structure of the buildings, board-and-care residents must be:

1. Ambulatory. This does not mean that they might not use an assistive device such as cane, walker or wheelchair. It does mean that they can shift themselves from bed to wheelchair and back again. They must be able to evacuate the building without assistance in the event of emergency. The staff is not large enough or trained for repeated transfers.

2. Continent. The staff expects "accidents," but they prefer residents to be basically continent.
3. Not more than mildly confused. The advanced elderly who are "forgetful," or who are in the very early stages of senile dementia are accepted. The staff will aid residents with such tasks as handling money, dressing and the dozens of other small details of day-to-day life. They are neither equipped nor licensed for extremely confused patients who might become combative or pose a danger to themselves or others. Although they watch over residents, they cannot restrain persistent wanderers who constantly leave the grounds and are unable to return.
4. Self-medicating. Only doctors or licensed nurses can dispense medications. A board-and-care facility can store a resident's medication and make it available at the appropriate time. It can watch while pills are consumed and ensure that the remainder are returned. It cannot actually dispense, pour or inject individual medications.
5. In reasonably good health. These facilities are not prepared to treat individuals who need nursing care. Many board-and-care establishments require a doctor's certificate that their level of care is appropriate.

## THE DENVER STUDY

In 1983, the Denver Research Institute did a study of elderly board-and-care residents and found:

31% had physical impairments that restricted activity

56% needed assistance in cleaning their rooms

46% needed assistance in managing money

42% needed assistance in taking medications

26% needed assistance in bathing

Another study found that 71% of the residents were on medications. The average resident is a 70-year-old white female who is either widowed or never married. She will be a resident for three years and will leave the facility once a week but will only travel four blocks.

## TYPES OF RESIDENTS

Board and care does not cater exclusively to the elderly, but also to the mentally disabled and the mentally retarded. In almost all jurisdictions, the mentally retarded are housed in group homes specifically oriented toward their needs. However, those states that do license board and care may grant a license for care to the elderly, care to the mentally disabled, or a mixed license where residents in both categories may be accepted.

The National Association of Residential Care Facilities 1989 Directory (NARCF) lists the following:

| Type of Facility | No. of Facilities | No. of Beds |
|---|---|---|
| Elderly only | 10,067 | 264,534 |
| Mentally disabled | 11,485 | 93,564 |
| Mentally retarded | 2,136 | 18,541 |
| Foster care | 3,903 | 11,865 |
| Mixed | 13,790 | 174,333 |
| Totals | 41,381 | 562,837 |

Note that while NARCF reports 41,381 facilities, the House Committee on Aging estimated that more than 68,000 exist. This difference of 26,619 is a minimum estimate of the number of unlicensed board-and-care establishments that operate throughout the country. While some states do not license this level of care at all, even those that do are not zealous in investigating the unlicensed. There are also many small foster-care homes that do not fall within license requirements, while conversely there are very large mixed-level nursing homes that fall under different licensing requirements and so are not counted here.

# WHAT ARE THESE PLACES LIKE?

The average board-and-care home houses 24 residents in a large modified building that is 43 years old. There are 16 bedrooms in the establishment, with fire protection that usually consists of smoke detectors. There are eight employees, one of whom probably lives on the premises. None of the staff has had formal instruction in the field but has received on-the-job training. The average cost is $8,000 a year, but many of the residents are on some form of government entitlement program.

Although small establishments far outnumber the large, more board-and-care beds are located in the larger facilities. The bigger homes tend to be nonprofit institutions sponsored by religious or fraternal organizations. Such facilities often have long waiting lists.

This industry is truly a "mom and pop" business since two-thirds of all establishments are owned by a single individual or a couple.

Although Canada has Universal Health Care paid through its Medicare program, a flourishing private rest home business has sprung up in provinces such as Ontario. The private Canadian facilities charge patients from $20 to $50 a day (in Canadian dollars), while the balance is paid by the province.

# COSTS

The rate for board and care can range from a low based on Social Security benefits to a high of $3,000 or more a month.

The cost range is so wide that it is difficult to establish definite fee patterns. A general guideline for any geographic area would be a daily rate that is half of the usual skilled nursing home charge for that locality.

The fees for residents in board-and-care homes whose charges are paid by a state entitlement program will be less than those paid by the general public. These programs, including Medicaid, reimburse facilities on a flat per diem allowable cost basis. These fees are so low that they are often at the break-even point or below for the facility. With a healthy mix of private and public residents, the board-and-care home will be profitable. If, for reasons of location or appearance, the home has a preponderance of entitlement residents with low reimbursement rates, the services are apt to be less.

In choosing a board-and-care facility, it would be helpful to know the approximate mix of private versus public residents.

# CHAPTER 16

# BOARD-AND-CARE PROBLEMS: "A National Tragedy"

## How Bad Are They?

Media reports, public perceptions and general outcries against the board-and-care industry approximate the deluge of criticism directed against nursing homes 20 years ago.

On March 9, 1989, the late Claude Pepper, who was then Chairman of the House Subcommittee on Health and Long-Term Care, said about board and care, "Abuse is so broad and systemic as to be evident in every state of the union." Congressman Pepper then narrated a slide show for the committee that included photographs of residents bound to wheelchairs or lying on the floor, and rest homes without fire safety equipment. "Neither the states nor the federal government, which together spend $7 billion annually on these facilities, have evidenced any real concern for their residents' safety," he went on to say.

"It is frightening how little we know about board-and-care homes," John Heinz of Pennsylvania, the ranking Republican on the Senate Special Committee on Aging, said on the same date. "This is an industry out of sight, out of mind, and out of control."

After the March 1989 hearings, the House Subcommittee on Health and Long-term Care issued a report, "Board and Care Homes in America: A National Tragedy." This report indicated that there were hundreds of cases of reported abuse, ranging from sexual abuse to theft of personal needs allowance, with the most prevalent abuses listed as mismanagement and malnutrition.

152

# WHY

The basic framework for this industry's problems lies in its history, its recent phenomenal growth and the lack of adequate federal or state regulation. In days past, small boarding homes were often the residences of spinster school teachers, widows and lonely men. Large homes were converted to this use to satisfy a dual need: extra income for the owner and housing for those on limited income and without family. As the residents aged, it was a small and benign step for the owners to provide the little extra care they needed.

Another important factor contributing to the growth of these establishments was the creation in 1965 of Medicare and the joint federal-state partnership of Medicaid (MediCal in California). There was a strong consumer movement to correct nursing home abuses, and federal regulations were promulgated with that aim. The states, in order to receive Medicaid reimbursement, were forced to adopt these nursing home standards. They formed inspection teams and regulatory groups, usually within state departments of health. Rest homes generally could not meet these new requirements for medical care and standards for fire safety, so they converted to board-and-care facilities, a step below nursing homes. These homes thus escaped the protective provisions designed for nursing homes. They are not covered under any other federal regulations and have only spotty and usually inadequate state supervision.

To complicate their weak underpinnings, this segment of the housing continuum has enjoyed phenomenal growth. When states reduced their hospital census of mental patients by an average of 73% between 1969 and 1987, many of these individuals were placed in board and care. Another large group of residents became eligible for board and care after the passage in January 1974 of the federally administered Supplemental Security Income Program (SSI). SSI superseded several other state and federal programs designed for old age assistance, aid to the blind and aid to the permanently and totally disabled. Many board-and-care operators were willing to accept SSI (as supplemented in many states) as full payment for their charges.

This influx of new residents into sometimes under-financed facilities run by weak management shook the burgeoning industry. Some owners sold out to unscrupulous and venal operators who milked the unregulated homes. Others stumbled on, unable to upgrade their buildings or services because of lack of capital. The good board-and-care facilities continued caring for their residents, but often went unnoticed amid the highly publicized problems of the others.

# WHAT HAPPENED TO
# THE REGULATIONS?

## FEDERAL

The federal government is able to impose stringent regulations on skilled nursing homes because of the financial power of their direct reimbursements. Although federal Medicare funds pay only 2% of nursing home charges, Medicaid pays more than half of all such fees. Social Security benefits and SSI do pay for a great many board-and-care charges, but only indirectly, as these funds go directly to the individual who in turn endorses them over to the facility. It is this difference in payment method that makes federal regulation so difficult.

### THE KEYS AMENDMENT

In the 1970s, a series of tragic fires resulted in a public outcry over board-and-care facilities. In 1976, Representative Martha Keys of Kansas offered an amendment to the Social Security Act that established standards for any institution, foster home or group living arrangement in which a significant number of SSI recipients lived. The states were required to certify annually to the Department of Health and Human Services that they had complied with the Keys amendment.

The amendment had several shortcomings that defeated its purpose. It did not provide any funding to help the states increase inspections or even to locate board-and-care homes. In addition, its penalties cut residents' benefits, and to many this seemed like punishing the victim for allowing himself to be robbed. It also meant that the states would be placed in the position of transferring these residents onto state entitlement programs and placing them in other institutions.

The states retaliated by quarreling over definitions within the legislation. At present, the amendment is deemed unenforceable.

### THE RINALDO AMENDMENT

In 1981 Congress, through the Rinaldo Amendment, expanded the state nursing home ombudsman program to include responding to complaints from residents of board-and-care homes. However, no additional funds were provided to the states for these additional responsibilities.

Prior regulations and funding through the Older American's Act required each state to establish a Nursing Home Ombudsman to receive patient complaints. An ombudsman has the power to enter any nursing home, demand records, interview patients and staff and investigate in other ways. If necessary, he or she can call on other state agencies for aid or enforcement.

The attempt to expand the Ombudsman program to board and care did not work. In 1987 the AARP, in conjunction with the National Association of State Units on Aging, and the Senate Special Committee on Aging, surveyed all state ombudsmen. Results from 48 states indicated that most ombudsmen believed it was important to visit board-and-care homes; however, more than half believed that they had not been successful in maintaining their presence in those facilities.

## STATE REGULATION OF BOARD AND CARE

The attempts by the states to regulate board and care have created a patchwork quilt that would delight the Mad Hatter. A 1985 study by JRB Associates identified 39 different program titles and 65 different size criteria utilized for state licensing. The General Accounting Office found widespread confusion among the states as to exactly what constitutes a board-and-care home, how to deal with unlicensed homes and how to use available sanctions to correct problems without harming the residents.

## IDENTIFICATION AND LICENSING

Before any regulations can be implemented, the facilities must be identified and licensed. This in itself presents a problem for several reasons:

The borderline cases. A boarding house may begin to provide protective oversight for a few long-time older residents. When these individuals leave or die, the homes revert to their usual services. An SRO hotel that serves primarily the elderly is another typical example. The hotel might provide or arrange for meals and housekeeping and gradually begin to offer other "helpful" services to frail residents. The question arises, when does the boarding house or hotel cross the line into the realm of board and care?

Loose state regulations. A home may be unlicensed simply because the existing laws do not specifically require it to be.

Lack of capital. A common reason to hide from licensing is financial problems in meeting state standards. The cost of fire safeguards such as sprinkler systems or fire escapes is typically mentioned. Many smaller homes just do not have the capital to invest, nor are they able to borrow for structural improvements based on projected income.

Number of residents. Many states, financially unable to inspect every small operation that cares for a few people, write their laws to exclude the tiny facilities. Abuse can occur as readily with two people as 200.

Confusion. There is confusion about exactly what the phrase "protective oversight" means. Does a staff member have to be physically present and awake all night? Is the helpful owner of a small boarding house providing protective oversight?

Provisional licenses. Many board-and-care homes have been operating on provisional licenses for years, unable to meet standards, applying for extensions on requirements or being grandfathered in. Authorities are often hesitant to close an otherwise competent facility whose beds they need.

In 1981 the State of Maryland undertook "Operation Identification." It matched computer tapes from the Social Security Administration, the Veteran's Administration and its own Welfare Department to locate addresses where several benefit checks were sent. It was able to identify 200 unlicensed board-and-care homes in Baltimore alone. However, it did not have the funds to pursue the matter further.

Maryland also sent out letters to all hospital discharge planners and social workers to obtain their help in identifying unlicensed board-and-care homes. It received one reply.

Studies indicate that homes that house predominantly public-supported residents have twice as many serious violations as those that serve self-pay residents. The states still continue to find serious problems in their licensed homes including physical abuse, unsanitary conditions, lack of medical attention and deadly combinations of these that actually kill residents. It can only be assumed that conditions are more severe in unlicensed and uninspected facilities.

In Ohio recently, a state health department nurse accidentally discovered residents in an unlicensed home that were not receiving adequate food, were covered with lesions and bedsores and had unattended chronic conditions.

# GENERAL PROBLEMS

The board-and-care industry distinctly reflects class structure in this country. This division creates one group of facilities for the affluent and middle-class and another for the poor. Board-and-care homes can be found that are opulent, staffed with trained individuals, surrounded by physical amenities and serve gourmet food. Other facilities have become society's warehouse for its older poor and afflicted. There are homes where excessive weight gain is a problem, while in others malnutrition is a threat.

There are other problems.

The industry's roots are in small boarding homes and marginal nursing homes. This lack of a strong financial base means that they are often unable to upgrade their facilities. Social workers and state inspectors are often aware of deficiencies but are unable to close the home because they need the beds. As an individual facility continues to deteriorate physically, so does its ability to attract self-pay residents. As its beds are filled with those on various entitlement programs, payments to the home are pegged at or near cost. With these low payment schedules, the home is further precluded from upgrading its facilities, and thus deterioration is perpetuated.

There are no standards for staff training. Personnel do not have any formal training in caring for confused residents, aiding with ADLs, or such basic procedures as the Heimlich maneuver.

Small is good, but too small is not good. In order to keep a facility from appearing institutional, 20 to 30 board-and-care residents are considered the optimum number. Facilities larger than this tend to resemble nursing homes, while those considerably smaller have their own distinct problems. A tiny home is apt to be a family enterprise with Mom doing the cooking, Dad the chores, and daughter the housekeeping. Recreational activities and social intervention on behalf of the residents are either forgotten or lost in the grinding work schedule. These families are often beset with burnout due to seven-day-a-week responsibilities without respite.

Inappropriate placements or changes in a resident's functional status can cause problems. Through naiveté, love or greed, some family members of the elderly who are involved in the placement decision will upgrade the functional status of their loved one. This can be because of wishful thinking, remembrance of how things once were, or an attempt to keep their relative from a higher and more expensive level of care.

An untrained staff is not able to notice subtle changes that might signal a loss of function. It is doubtful that drug reactions would be recognized or that the early stages of urinary tract infections would be noticed.

An inappropriate placement or change in physical or mental functions is compounded if the owner-operator needs income and discourages resident discharges.

Inadequate capitalization, untrained personnel and a host of residents in the wrong care category can all lead to poor delivery of essential services. This can be readily seen in the lack of recreational opportunities in substandard homes. In these facilities, residents are seen numbly seated before television sets for the majority of their waking hours. These understaffed homes have neither the time nor the ability to integrate their residents into any meaningful community programs the area might offer.

# CHAPTER 17

# HOW TO SELECT A BOARD-AND-CARE FACILITY: And Monitor the New Resident

## AN ADVOCATE

The prospective board-and-care resident has reached a point in life when independent living is not practical. There might be any number of reasons for this, but one probable result is a partial limitation of physical mobility and the inability to drive a car. These restrictions inhibit the resident's ability to make extensive tours of potential facilities. It is in this search that the elderly now require an advocate to help survey possible homes.

The resident's advocate might be a family member, friend, minister or social worker. It is his or her function to reduce the choice to a manageable number by weeding out the inappropriate and inadequate.

*It is imperative that the resident participate in the final choice.* If the resident does not take part in the decision-making process, he will feel abandoned, unloved and warehoused. These emotional conflicts will generate resistance, depression and impair acceptance of any facility. The determination to begin a search for a proper board-and-care home should be made jointly, just as the final determination of which one to enter should also be by mutual agreement.

There are three other important factors to consider *before the search begins:*

1. Choose the right facility the first time. Although cognitive functions may not have diminished, many elderly at this stage in life are not flexible in their adaptation to new environments. This factor, along with the problems inherent in the industry, make the proper choice doubly important. Be sure the facility you select will be adequate, because

moving the resident later will be deleterious to his physical and mental health.

2. Consider the proper level of care. This is not the time in life for the resident to be "challenged." If he is not going to be able to function properly within the framework provided, the care level should be seriously reconsidered. Obviously, the resident's primary care physician should be consulted. As an example, if the resident has a deteriorating chronic condition, perhaps a custodial facility that is part of a skilled nursing home complex should be considered. Since shifts of residency are upsetting, a change from the custodial wing to the nursing home floor in the same facility would not be as traumatic as a complete move. Remember, too, that if you choose this alternative, the institutional atmosphere will be more apparent than in the smaller home-like board-and-care establishment.

3. Keep it simple. It is the advocate's task to screen facilities and not to provide a mammoth menu of alternatives. Two or three choices, at most, are adequate and are less confusing.

## LET THE SEARCH BEGIN

If the prospective resident has been active in church or fraternal organizations that sponsor such facilities, these homes should be investigated first. Many religious, ethnic and social groups are very active in this field and run fine establishments for their elderly. This type of environment offers almost instant socialization, a concerned board of directors and, unfortunately, the longest waiting lists in the industry.

Physicians with a high percentage of geriatric patients, hospital discharge planners, clergy and social workers are excellent sources of information. If you wish to enlarge your scope of exploration, contact your local Area Agency on Aging, the State Department on Aging, or the state or national office of the National Association of Residential Care Facilities.

In any event, your State Department on Aging should be contacted to find out which agency is involved in licensing these facilities. The state agency that handles inspections and regulation of nursing homes and board-and-care facilities is usually within the Department of Health. They will be able to provide information regarding licensing requirements and, if your state is well regulated, copies of any home's last inspection report.

## THE FIRST STEPS

1. Try a windshield inspection. A slow drive-by will give you the first clue. If the building's exterior is run down, needs paint and mainte-

nance and the grounds are not well tended, save time—keep going. A home that does not maintain its outside isn't going to do a very good job inside either.

2.  Visit unannounced. You are not interested in having tea and crumpets with the administrator. You want to see them as they usually are. You want to view housekeeping, staff and resident reactions, and cooking preparations, when visitors are not expected.

3.  First impressions do count. The initial greeting at the front door during an unannounced visit will reveal a great deal. A surprised and sour reception probably indicates a surly attitude toward residents. A room full of sloppily dressed, uncommunicative residents silently watching television reflects a sterile environment with little resident care.

4.  Who's talking? The verbal and physical interaction between residents, staff and visitors should reveal hidden elements of hostility or even fear. Studies on board and care indicate that most residents are far more concerned about their interaction with peers than they are with physical amenities. If residents appear happy and satisfied, they probably are.

5.  Fire safety is of the utmost importance! The average board-and-care home is apt to be housed in an older wooden building. It will always have some fire protection devices such as smoke detectors or even barrier doors—but often will not have a sprinkler system. The home without a sprinkler system may have a provisional license, might have been grandfathered into licensure, be of nonconforming use or operating under loose regulations. Whatever the reason, the fire hazards are immense in these institutions, not only because of their construction, but because of the forgetfulness of their smoking residents. It is foolhardy to voluntarily reside in a facility without a sprinkler system.

6.  Run a credit check. The smaller board-and-cares are often run by a family or small corporation. If they have difficulty in paying their bills, the residents will suffer from staff shortages or poor food.

# A CHECKLIST

If the home you are interested in has passed the primary steps, you are now ready for the guided tour. Watch carefully for the following:

1.  The Other Residents. Take a quick census of the other residents. Do they seem to be of an age or mix that will allow your resident to fit in? For example, if the prospective resident is in her seventies, and the bulk of the other residents are far younger, the meld might not be beneficial.

2.  Halls and Doors. Are the halls wide enough for wheelchairs? Do all exits have ramps? All halls should have rails for those who need sup-

port during ambulation. If interior stairs are present, is the resident able to safely go up and down?

3.  Common Rooms. Are they attractive, well lit and adequate for the number of residents? Is there a specific room for recreational activities, with card tables, hobby space and games? Are large-print books and magazines available?

    Fluorescent lights should not be used since they flicker and can cause headaches in the elderly. Color perception in the aged is also affected, so that busy rug patterns and pastel colors are confusing and disorienting. All furniture should be devoid of sharp edges in case of falls. Easy chairs and couches should have firm support without deep seat cushions that make rising difficult.

4.  Residents' Rooms. Although a private room would be preferred, occupancy by more than two people would be unacceptable. Each resident must have at least 150 square feet of space and be allowed to bring all or part of his own furnishings. The room should contain a bed, dresser, side table, desk and easy chair. Adequate closet space and lighting are important items to check. The average 80-year-old needs several times more light than a 20-year-old, but is also vulnerable to glare.

    The administration should be asked about roommate transfers (if applicable) and the home's policy on private telephones, televisions and security arrangements for personal belongings.

5.  Bathrooms. The bathroom should be easily accessible to the bedroom and must have a nightlight. It must be located so that the individuals using a wheelchair or walker would not have difficulty gaining entrance. A raised toilet with grab-bars is helpful, while grab-bars and a non-skid surface in the tub or shower are an absolute necessity.

6.  Food. The importance of good food attractively presented to any group of people whose lives are circumscribed cannot be overemphasized. Mealtime is an hour of socialization that is anticipated by all residents. The way and attitude with which a meal is served and small amenities such as in-season flower bouquets, can do a great deal to enhance the experience.

    Food should be prepared from fresh meat and vegetables rather than heated from institutional-size cans. Diets should be well rounded with three-week menu cycles and should include fresh fruits and vegetables that are in season.

    Special diets should be available if directed, and snacks should be served in the afternoon and evening.

    A staff member should surreptitiously take a head count to see that all residents are present for the meal, check on anyone missing and take notice if any individual is not eating properly. A problem to watch for in the understaffed home is the scheduling of all meals within one eight-hour work shift. Compressing cooking, serving and cleanup into this time frame may be efficient for management, but it is not helpful to the residents.

7. Housekeeping and Laundry. How often are linens changed, and what are the arrangements for personal laundry? Is the general housekeeping adequate? Are the halls free of blockage by buckets, slippery surfaces or any other impediments that might cause someone to fall? Is the resident responsible for keeping her own room and, if so, can she receive aid if necessary?

8. Recreation. Are meaningful recreational activities provided? If they are, is a calendar of events posted prominently?

   A board-and-care home of 30 or fewer residents will not have a full-time recreational therapist, but it should have someone who visits the facility on a regular, if part-time, basis.

9. Transportation. Transportation should be provided not only for doctors' appointments but also for shopping, church and other community activities.

10. Emergencies. Are there call bells in each resident's room and all the bathrooms? Is someone on duty 24 hours a day to monitor any calls? What ambulance service and hospital are used in the event of an emergency?

11. Medications and Health. Discuss in full detail the home's method of tracking each resident's medication. Evaluate this information against the requirements of the entering resident.

    If the new resident has difficulty in performing activities of daily living, determine what aid the staff will provide for these functions.

# THE CONTRACT (LEASE OR RESIDENT AGREEMENT)

In addition to the contract (lease), the home may have a resident's handbook containing house standards and rules. Both documents should be carefully reviewed to ensure that the proper services are to be provided and that the day-to-day operating rules don't conflict with the new resident's desires and lifestyle. At the same time, the administration should present each applicant with a copy of the "Resident's Bill of Rights," which will also be prominently displayed at some central location (see Appendix for sample copy).

The contract should carefully outline all financial arrangements. It must indicate:

* the monthly rate for room and board, including the advance deposit, which should not exceed the first month's charges plus two additional months.

- the provisions and timeframe for refund of any unused funds because of death or discharge.
- any additional charges for extra services to be performed. [Personal laundry or extensive help with ADLs might be two areas calling for additional charges.]
- the holding period for a vacated room. If the resident needs hospitalization, or should leave temporarily for any reason, the room should be held for a minimum of three months. The charge for this period should be less than the daily rate since meals are not consumed.

## MONITORING THE RESIDENT

It is very possible that the new board-and-care resident has been living independently prior to the recent move. This person is going to be acutely aware of the loss of freedom that comes with group living. It is a difficult time, filled with adaptations that are often difficult for the elderly. The new resident needs a friend, a trusted benefactor, an advocate to continue to help in this transition.

There is also the possibility that a mistake has been made in the selection of the facility, which may be discovered only by follow-up visits.

There are five steps in the board-and-care monitoring visit.

Step 1: Vary your visiting day and hour. Many board-and-care residents do not have any visitors; therefore, your arrivals and departures will be noted by the staff. If they expect you every Thursday at 2:00 PM, you may rest assured that your well-groomed resident will meet you at the door to escort you to her spotless room. The visits must be staggered in such a manner that they overlap staff shift changes. The day crew may be great, but Count Dracula may handle the desk at night.

Step 2: Eat a meal. Anyone who has spent time in any type of institution is aware of the importance of food. The resident's advocate should share a few of these meals as a method of quality control. Keep in mind that if the facility caters primarily to the elderly, portions need not be as large as those served at a college athletic table. A sophisticated kitchen will also choose meat entrees that are appropriate. A thick steak might be enjoyable to a 55-year-old, but for anyone with denture problems an easier-to-consume tender pot roast might be preferable.

Step 3: Continue observing staff and residents. As everyone acclimates to your presence, their conversation and attitudes will relax. If residents remain subdued and fearful or if the staff is condescending or disrespectful to the residents, deep problems may exist.

Step 4: Are housekeeping standards maintained? It is not uncommon for a busy staff to disengage call bells and block exits in order to make their lives easier. These are dangerous practices that should be reported immediately.

Are the beds made? Is there a smell in the halls? What about the bathrooms? One glance should answer these questions. Remember that a single unmade bed may have a valid explanation, just as an accident in the hall might be a temporary problem. It is the consistency of general housekeeping that indicates if a home is well maintained. Poor housekeeping is only the outward sign of deeper problems within that particular home.

Step 5: Check your resident. Since you vary your visiting days and times, the staff has no reason to expect you at a certain hour and groom the resident accordingly. Physical appearance reveals the extent of general care. Is her hair combed? Are her clothes clean and coordinated? Make a quick room check to see that linens have been changed and personal belongings are in order.

Through conversations with the resident and staff it must be determined if there is proper socialization. This involves participation in at least some recreational programs and talking with a roommate, if there is one.

Make a check of the medications to see that the proper number of pills has been taken since the prescription was ordered and arrange for refills, if necessary. Find out if medical appointments have been scheduled and transportation arranged. Don't forget the hairdresser or barber.

The advocate must always be alert to the possibility that the resident's physical or mental condition has deteriorated to the point where this level of care is not appropriate. If such a decline is noticed, the search for a proper nursing home should begin before a crisis occurs.

# BOARD-AND-CARE SUMMARY

Board and care for the elderly exists under a variety of names, but is defined as those facilities that provide room and board combined with protective oversight. This supervision is nonmedical in nature, but should include assistance with some ADLs. The home should be involved with local support services, and should provide transportation and personal assistance in obtaining medical and social services for its residents.

This segment of the elderly housing continuum is often the answer for those who are alone and unable to live independently, but are not chronically disabled or so extremely confused that they must enter a skilled nursing home.

The wide range of cost for this housing varies from a low payable from monthly Social Security benefits to highs that can exceed $3,000 a month.

Many establishments house only a handful of residents in modified homes, while other custodial facilities have hundreds of beds.

Advocates of those elderly who have adequate monthly incomes can search and find the proper facilities, although they are warned to be careful in their selection. The less affluent elderly who must pay for this care from state entitlement programs, low Social Security benefits or SSI, may be relegated to homes that may not only be less than adequate, but potentially dangerous.

Our society has presently chosen not to address this problem and does not properly regulate and inspect these facilities. Even the few existing state regulations are primarily concerned with sanitation and physical plants rather than the quality of life. In addition, entitlement program funding for residents is often too low to place this industry on a healthy financial footing.

# CHAPTER 18

# SKILLED NURSING HOMES AND OTHER MEDICAL ALTERNATIVES

## MYTH AND REALITY

In our collective mind there are certain words that conjure feelings of dread, distaste and fear. Certainly, "nursing homes" are two such words.

It would be an understatement to say that this industry has had a bad press. Unfavorable newspaper and magazine articles and television exposés on the topic are legion. These horror stories become doubly poignant because we all fear that in a foreseeable future our friends, parents or spouses may be forced into one of "those places." Our repugnance prompts denial and discourages a thoughtful approach to the selection process. Even administrators of life-care projects are amazed that their prospective residents will often avoid or skip the nursing home tour during the sales presentation.

A first step in a rational approach to the decision and selection process is the realization that good nursing homes do exist, and they often offer intelligent, skilled and compassionate care to their residents. These facilities are often medically necessary, and they are occasionally a desirable alternative to home care that is either inadequate or physically and emotionally devastating to the care givers.

There are also nursing homes that must be avoided—facilities that provide such poor care that the morbidity and mortality rates of their patients increase in an alarming manner. These poor nursing homes, which are usually characterized by inadequate staffing, are fertile ground for unacceptable bed sores, abuse of physical and chemical restraints and a lack of proper nursing treatments. In 1989, New York State inspectors found a nursing home where 68% of the patients were restrained, 13% had bed sores and 36% were contractured (meaning they had a permanent stiffening of the joints from inactivity). They also concluded that this home did not meet federal and state standards for residents' rights, infection control, nutrition, nursing services, administration of drugs and patient care management. However, this huge list of deficiencies resulted only in fines rather than loss of license.

Consigning a member of the frail elderly to such an establishment will shorten his or her life span radically, not to mention the poor quality of life during those remaining months or years.

## WHO'S GOING TO GO?

There are 1.5 million Americans in nursing homes at any given time. The optimist might say that breaks down to only 5% of those over 65, while the pessimist will note that more than 44% of those over 65 will spend some time in a nursing home. The majority of nursing home stays will be for a short period after an acute care hospitalization for the purpose of stabilization and rehabilitation. Only 13% of those over 65 will spend a year or more in a nursing home, but one quarter of those over 85 will reside permanently in those facilities. It must also be remembered that this over-85 age group is increasing three times faster than the population as a whole.

Cost containment policies by Medicare have caused acute care hospitals to discharge patients who are weaker and sicker than in years past. These patients will often need several weeks of skilled nursing home care and therapy before returning home. More than half of the patients who enter a nursing home will do so directly from their own homes. These are most apt to be the individuals who will need this care on a long-term basis as the final stage of their elderly housing continuum.

There is a continuing myth that we warehouse our elderly in nursing homes for convenience's sake. This is simply not true. The average nursing home patient is an 81-year-old white widow who is confused and incontinent. She suffers from two or more chronic medical conditions. This individual needs constant monitoring and care far beyond the ordinary family's ability to provide.

# A QUICK LOOK AT ELDERLY MEDICAL FACILITIES

## ACUTE-CARE HOSPITALS

These facilities can range in size from the two-dozen-bed local community hospital to the huge multibuilding medical center affiliated with a medical school that offers a wide range of specialized services. Patients are admitted to these hospitals because of a sudden illness or a rapid deterioration of a chronic disease. The level of activity at these institutions is very high and often harried. The elderly, especially those who become confused, can be easily overwhelmed by this milieu. For cost reasons, acute care hospitals attempt to discharge patients as soon as possible. This often means a nursing home stay for further stabilization and/or rehabilitation.

## REHABILITATION CENTERS

Rehab centers are often part of a medical center but can also be separate institutions. Admission is usually directly from the acute care hospital on the recommendation of the attending physician and a team of rehab specialists. Although these centers treat a wide spectrum of rehab problems, younger elderly who are stroke victims are especially good candidates for their intensive physical, occupational and speech therapy programs. The high goals of these centers require great patient stamina, and thus the frail elderly are not always good candidates; however, this does not mean that these patients can't benefit from nursing home rehab programs.

## GERIATRIC ASSESSMENT UNITS

Many of the larger metropolitan hospitals have established outpatient Geriatric Assessment Units. These interdisciplinary teams perform a complete physical and psychological evaluation of the patient and an evaluation of the family for their caretaking abilities. Neuropsychologic testing is performed and can often clarify the presence and magnitude of dementia.

These units can be of extreme importance in two areas. Although more than half of all senile dementia is of the Alzheimer's type (SDAT), nearly half is not. At present, Alzheimer's can be absolutely diagnosed only at the time of autopsy. Although Alzheimer's disease is incurable, other types of senile dementia are reversible and so great care must be taken before anyone is labeled with SDAT.

These units can often be helpful to families who are making the initial nursing home decision. Their trained geriatric social workers know exactly what support services a community can provide, and a comparison of this availability plus family resources against patient needs can help a concerned family to make this choice.

## HOSPICE

A hospice is not a specific place, but a philosophy of care for the terminally ill. There are presently more than 1,800 hospice programs operating in the United States and Canada. Only 535 of these programs are Medicare approved, since the remainder do not have in-patient facilities for their patients. For those programs that are Medicare approved, much of the cost is paid by that health plan.

A hospice program may operate through a home care agency, a community hospital, a skilled nursing home or under the umbrella of other health care agencies. The better programs will include skilled nursing care and physicians trained in pain control and will offer homemaker services and bereavement teams that work with both patient and family.

The Connecticut Hospice of Branford, Connecticut, which began operation in 1974, is the oldest in this country. Its philosophy is typical of the hospice approach:

1.  To help patients live out their lives as fully and as comfortably as possible.
2.  To support the family as an integral part of the hospice care.
3.  To enable patients to remain at home as long as possible.

The typical hospice patient will be over 65 and suffer from a terminal cancer. He or she often will have gone through an aggressive treatment program at an acute-care hospital but now wishes to die with dignity without further extraordinary medical efforts. The program attempts to keep the patient home, with extensive medical help and volunteers, as long as possible. As the terminal stage nears, the patient will transfer to the hospice in-patient unit.

The in-patient units have a one-to-one nurse ratio, and no life-saving machinery or resuscitation orders. Oxygen is provided as a palliative measure, and a pharmacist makes daily rounds with the medical personnel to aid in pain control. They are very successful in controlling pain with drugs taken orally, which results in less confusion to the patient.

Hospice offers an answer to the terminally ill who have a known prognosis. The program works for cancer patients whose disease has a certain predictability. It will not work with the frail elderly who suffer from several chronic conditions and may die either tomorrow or two years from now.

# NURSING HOMES

Medical personnel may refer to three types of nursing homes: custodial, intermediate and skilled. Custodial homes (rest homes, etc.) are for individuals who are in basically good health and who are ambulatory and continent, but do require extensive services and protective oversight. These residents do not require daily medical care. This type of facility was covered extensively in the chapters on board and care.

Intermediate nursing homes also usually require their patients to be able to self-transfer, be mostly continent and not require extensive medical or nursing treatments.

Depending on the owner's orientation, an intermediate nursing home may lean toward the custodial facility or, in the opposite direction, toward the skilled nursing home. As a consequence, many of these institutions are neither fish nor fowl. The subject is further complicated by the fact that many nursing homes have dual licensure and are certified for both intermediate and skilled nursing home patients. In the larger homes, over 120 beds, these patients are often segregated by wing or floor. Smaller facilities may be mixed, with both levels of patient residing in the same unit. Because of this mix, the placement of a patient may often appear to be arbitrary. As a consequence, recent federal legislation has ignored the intermediate designation and only recognizes skilled nursing homes. Some states have required intermediate only facilities to either upgrade their services to skilled, or accept licensure as custodial facilities.

# SKILLED NURSING HOMES

Along with so many other topics in the senior housing continuum, skilled nursing homes go by many names, both in the United States and in Canada. A telephone directory search will reveal listings for convalescent homes, chronic-care facilities, health care facilities, nursing centers, skilled nursing homes and others. (See Chapter 10 for a discussion of nursing homes in life care.) The Canadian government officially recognizes two types of nursing homes: residential homes, which correspond to the United States' custodial or board and care facilities, and extended care facilities, which are the equivalent of the United States' skilled nursing homes.

Federal and state regulations define skilled nursing homes "as health care facilities with continuous licensed nurse coverage with the capabilities of providing around-the-clock nursing treatments as ordered by the patient's physicians."

It must be noted, once again, that some nursing homes will choose, for financial reasons, not to be Medicare/Medicaid approved. However, the state regulations concerning the operation of these homes will be the same as for those that are approved.

# THE STAFF

## THE DOCTORS

Each nursing home is required to have a **medical director** who is a licensed physician. This doctor is in charge of all medical matters within the facility and provides liaison between the medical staff and the administration. The medical director, except in very large nursing homes, usually has a private practice and will also treat many of the residents. He or she must be available on an emergency basis if a patient's doctor cannot be reached.

Each patient will have an **attending physician,** who is the doctor responsible for that resident's primary care. The attending physician may or may not have been the patient's doctor before admission, as this is often dependent on whether that particular doctor has admitting privileges at that nursing home.

If the patient's primary care physician does not have admitting privileges, a list of approved doctors will be provided.

## THE NURSES

Federal and state regulations stipulate how many registered nurses, licensed practical nurses and nurses' aides must be working for each shift. The federal regulations require an RN to be on duty during the daylight hours, while many state regulations take this further and require RN coverage 24 hours a day.

**Registered nurses** are graduates of approved courses that may be two, three or four years in length. **Licensed Practical Nurses** (called licensed vocational nurses in some states) are graduates of approved courses usually a year in length. RNs and LPNs have about the same clinical training, although RNs, particularly from the four-year-degree programs, have a stronger academic background.

Because of the nature of the majority of nursing home tasks, it is very difficult to differentiate the RN from the LPN in this milieu. While their differences in training and responsibility are more apparent in acute-care hospitals, they are less so in the skilled nursing home.

**Nurse's aides** (often called nursing assistants) must now be certified by the state. These short training programs, usually two weeks in duration, are given by the individual nursing homes.

Each nursing unit, usually consisting of 30 patients, will have a **charge nurse** who is responsible for that shift. All nurses, of all types for all shifts, are the responsibility of the **director of nursing.**

## THE THERAPISTS

**Physical, occupational** and **speech** therapists must be available for patient sessions as ordered by the physician. The physical therapist will work with patients to help them regain or retain the use of certain muscle groups. Occupational therapists teach patients how to adapt themselves to perform the routine activities of daily living. Speech therapists commonly work with stroke patients who are aphasic (can't speak) or who have a swallowing dysfunction.

Medicare/Medicaid approved nursing homes must have a **Recreational therapist** on the staff and publish a calendar of scheduled recreational events.

## OTHER PERSONNEL

The **nursing home administrator,** who is licensed by the state, is the individual who is ultimately responsible for everything that happens in the facility.

The **social worker** can be very helpful in assisting families in establishing Medicare/Medicaid eligibility and in discharge planning. This individual should be aware of what community services are available and whether or not they have the facilities to help a home-going patient. The social worker should also be able to counsel and support families during emotionally difficult times.

# NURSING HOME OWNERSHIP

Since 1974 there has been a 38% increase in nursing home beds, but even with this expansion these facilities are averaging 92% occupancy rates. Their 1.6 million beds are divided among 25,000 different nursing homes, which are owned as follows:

| | |
|---|---|
| Nursing home chains | 41% |
| Other Private | 34% |
| Nonprofit | 20% |
| Governmental | 5% |

Nursing homes would appear to be big business, and one corporation, Beverly Enterprises Inc., does own nearly 700 facilities. However, the average nursing home is still a rather small unit except in the larger metropolitan areas.

Nonprofit nursing homes are those sponsored by religious, fraternal or other charitable groups. By definition, these organizations cannot make a profit, so that any excess funds are usually returned in the form of increased services. Since these facilities offer immediate socialization for members of their group and are run by benevolent sponsors, they are often fine institutions. Unfortunately, these positive factors create long waiting lists and a level of care that makes them more expensive than profit-making facilities.

Governmental nursing homes include those beds reserved in Veterans Administration hospitals, state "Old Soldier's Homes," and the last vestiges of county homes or other small mixes of publicly funded facilities.

# NURSING HOME COSTS

## HOW MUCH?

The average daily rate for a semiprivate room in a skilled nursing home varies from $101.91 in the Northeast to $67.89 in the South. Higher rates are found in urban areas. The state of New York estimates that the average daily rate in metropolitan New York City is $167 per day. On a national mean, the daily rate currently hovers above $80 per day and will soon reach $100.

These daily rates cover the cost of a semiprivate room (usually two patients to a room), board, basic nursing care and other routine services. Private rooms will usually cost $20 per day above the usual per diem rate. Also included in the daily rate will be recreational and social work functions and the use of the various therapy and examining rooms.

Some nursing homes may make additional charges for personal laundry, while all nursing homes will charge extra for a television, personal phones and beauty parlor use. Add-on charges may also include linen and diaper fees for incontinent patients and fees for patients who must be hand fed.

Physician, therapy and prescription charges will also be in addition to the daily rate. The patient's primary physician's charges will probably be covered under Medicare Part B, the therapists may be covered and drug charges will be paid by the individual.

Paradoxically, nonprofit nursing homes are usually 10% more expensive than profit-making institutions. This rate differential seems to be attributable to higher nursing staff requirements in the nonprofit facilities.

In the Canadian system, most provinces require that the nursing home patient pay a small daily rate of around $20 (Canadian) a day.

## WHO PAYS

The unfairness of nursing home payments is that they come directly from the pockets of the patient or her family, until she is impoverished and must turn to a welfare entitlement program.

One half of all nursing home patients pay all charges directly from their own or family funds. Forty-four percent of the patients are carried by Medicaid (a joint federal-state entitlement program). Medicare pays barely 2% of all nursing home fees, private long-term care insurance another 2%, with the small balance funded by the Veterans Administration or other state and local assistance programs.

An examination of annual health care costs reveals that for those over 65, 41% of their health care dollars are spent on nursing homes, even though only 5% of the elderly are residing in one at any given time.

The House Select Committee on Aging estimates that nursing home fees impoverish two-thirds of all single elderly and half of all couples within one year.

## MEDICARE

Most people are astonished when they discover that Medicare pays such a small portion of nursing home fees. Medicare, in its present form, was never designed for long-term care, and its stringent restrictions follow that philosophy.

If a nursing home stay is approved by Medicare, it will pay all allowable semiprivate room charges for the first 20 days, and from the 21st through 100th day any fees over a patient payment of $74 a day.

To qualify for Medicare, the patient must enter the nursing home within 30 days of an acute-care hospitalization for treatment of the same condition. The patient must require skilled nursing care on a daily basis that will improve his or her condition. Medicare will not pay for custodial care, and it interprets this in the broadest possible sense.

## MEDICAID

Medicaid is a health care entitlement program for those of low income. It is also known as Title 19, and, in California, as MediCal; Medicaid is not available in Arizona. Fifty-six percent of the cost of Medicaid is funded by the federal government, and the balance by the individual states. The program does pay for nursing home charges for those who qualify, and it does not have the onerous medical restrictions and limitations of Medicare. It is administered by the various states, usually through their welfare departments, and therefore eligibility requirements will vary within broad federal guidelines.

There are stringent asset and income restrictions for Medicaid entitlement. Most states will require single patients to pay all of their monthly income to the nursing home less a small monthly personal allowance of from $50 to $70. Medicaid will then pay the balance of any fees. Except for the patient's primary dwelling, and a few other minor items, all assets must be spent before there is Medicaid eligibility. The amount of allowed protected assets varies from state to state, but it is usually around $2,000 for single individuals. The state will usually file a lien against the primary dwelling, or require its sale if the nursing home stay is considered permanent.

Recent changes for married couples now allow the at-home spouse to retain the primary dwelling and from $12,000 to $60,000 in protected assets, depending on the state. The new federal guidelines also allow the at-home spouse to retain up to $1,500 per month in Social Security or other income and still have Medicaid eligibility.

Medicaid benefits will be denied if there have been transfers of assets within 30 months of application, or benefits will be denied for the dollar amount of such transfers divided into the average monthly nursing home rate. Certain intrafamily real estate transfers can be made under restricted conditions, but these should not be undertaken without professional advice.

A word of warning: The regulations concerning assets for the at-home spouse are new and have not been tested in court, nor in all cases have the states promulgated their complete rulings. Attempts to funnel assets into trusts or into the primary dwelling might be disallowed by appropriate state agencies.

## LONG-TERM CARE INSURANCE

Ordinary Medicare supplement insurance policies (Medigap policies) and other private plan policies do not pay for nursing home confinements—unless a specific long-term care policy is purchased.

In 1985, only 16 insurance companies provided these policies on a very restricted basis and fewer than 100,000 policies were outstanding. By 1990 their coverage had broadened and 105 companies were providing policies with more than one million outstanding.

These policies are sold in benefit increments of $10 a day, up to a maximum of $100 to $150 a day. Premiums are also calculated on the basis of age, waiting period from the time of admission, inflation riders, and the length of time benefits are paid.

As an example, according to the premium table for a major insurance company, a policy yielding $80 a day for a period of four years with a 5% inflation rider and a 20-day deductible or waiting period, would have premiums of:

$264 annually at age 50
$678.40 annually at age 60.
$1,172.80 annually at age 65
$2,171.20 annually at age 70
$6,512.80 annually at age 80

This plan would also pay up to $40 a day for home care or custodial care. A list of recommended coverage by these policies is included in the Appendix.

The figures speak for themselves: the cost of such insurance is reasonable if purchased at the age of 50, expensive for those on fixed income if bought at 70.

## POSSIBLE LIFE INSURANCE BENEFITS

In January 1990 the Prudential Life Insurance Company of America announced that it would pay full life insurance benefits to its policyholders who were terminally ill or permanently confined to a nursing home. Policyholders who have been in a nursing home for at least six months and have no expectation of discharge can elect to receive full benefits or monthly payments. This company's three million insured in the United States will have this option as soon as it is approved by the various states and in Canada. It is expected that other insurers will follow this competitive lead.

Prior to Prudential's move, several insurers offered similar benefits under accelerated-death benefit policies, but there were extra charges for these riders.

# CHAPTER 19

# NURSING HOME DECISIONS: When to Go, How to Choose, Monitoring and Complaints

## THE ENTRY DECISION

Society has created a host of ceremonies to mark various stages of life. Graduation, wedding and retirement all mark any individual's passage from one phase of life to another. However, there is no ceremony to mark entrance into a nursing home for what may be the final stage of the elderly housing continuum.

Prospective patients are often plagued with an acute sense of abandonment when faced with this alternative, while other family members respond with guilt. These emotional dynamics are often further complicated by a lack of clear-cut medical advice. The most attentive primary care physician can recommend drug and nursing regimens but is often not in a position to determine if a family or spouse is able to provide care on a day-to-day basis.

Guilt, in all its manifestations, is the most common emotion in the families of prospective nursing home patients. This guilt often manifests itself as anger, directed not only toward the patient, but also at other family members. All too often these feelings cause postponement of the nursing home entry as families attempt to adjust to a home-care situation of impossible dimensions. The prospective patient senses only the anger, and this increases the feeling of abandonment; or conversely the patient manipulates the guilt to her own ends, which further disrupts the family equilibrium.

The complicating factor in this emotional decision is that there are no clear guidelines for when to admit a family member to a nursing home. Most patients are admitted from their own homes and, in most cases, might have remained at home if proper home-care resources were available. If families have unlimited time and funds to devote to home care, most patients might stay at home.

From a practical viewpoint, home care often means daughter care. Or in the instance of surviving marriages, we find the frail caring for the frail. Home-health-care agencies can provide professional help, but at high cost.

Family members must realize that in many instances a nursing home placement is not only necessary, but beneficial to the patient.

Consider the following:

1.  Is the prospective patient receiving adequate care in the home? Love is not enough. The bedridden, confused or incontinent elder can be a very difficult member of any household. The combination of all three conditions may be truly daunting and difficult for the untrained to handle. Decubiti (bed sores), if untreated, can become incurable. The partially immobile elderly must be groomed, ambulated and aided with his or her activities of daily living.
2.  If the elderly person is living alone, has he or she exhibited certain danger signs? Has there been a marked change in personal appearance, a decrease in nutritional status or confusion? Eighteen percent of those over 70 say they cannot care for their own basic needs, and yet many of these individuals still live alone. Accidents, substance abuse, social isolation and depression are just a few problems faced by those living alone. There comes a time when even semi-independent living is actually dangerous for the elderly person.
3.  Has there been a careful assessment of care needs against what is available in the community? Two-thirds of homes with a patient at nursing home risk do not receive any community support services. These in-home community services are perhaps not available in the area, are beyond the economic reach of the family or have not been identified.
4.  Is the home care situation destroying the family? Today's society, with its mobility, dual careers and high divorce rate, has reduced the availability of home-care providers. Marriages can be torn asunder, and families can be broken if members attempt to force someone into this duty.

# BEFORE THE SEARCH BEGINS

The potential long-term care nursing home patient is unlikely to be energetic or mobile enough to conduct an active and intelligent search for herself. It is therefore probable that the selection will rest with another member of the family. In consideration of this, and with the knowledge that adjustment to nursing home life is difficult, it is essential that the following be considered:

1. Because of the shortage of nursing home beds and the importance of the selection process, the search should begin as far in advance as possible. Although medical prognosis of a chronic illness cannot be fine-tuned to a given day, week or month, a clear understanding of the possible future will allow plans to be formulated. This knowledge should allow a more leisurely search without frantic concern over waiting lists at desirable institutions.

2. The decision to place someone in a nursing home should be mutually arrived at by all primary family members. If at all possible, the prospective patient should be a party to this and every other major decision in the selection process.

3. An energetic member of the family should be selected as the patient's advocate. This individual will not only be the most active in the search but will also be responsible for any dealings with the physicians, administrators and nurses, and will be charged with monitoring the patient's care after admission.

4. It must be agreed that, after a careful consideration of all options, a nursing home placement is the best answer. It is imperative that all those involved support this decision.

5. Everyone, especially the prospective patient, must understand that the entry decision and the diligence with which the search will be made are indicative of the love and feeling everyone has for the patient and that these decisions were made after careful consideration.

# THE EIGHT STEPS—HOW TO CHOOSE A NURSING HOME

## STEP ONE: START YOUR LIST WITH MEDICARE/ MEDICAID APPROVED NURSING HOMES.

Approval by the Joint Commission of Accreditation of Hospitals (JCAH) is a definite plus, but not a prerequisite. JCAH approval is an expensive process and many good nursing homes do not bother to apply.

Although the patient may not receive any Medicare funds for the stay and may not be eligible for Medicaid entitlement, Medicare/Medicaid approved homes are recommended. Medicare eligibility may change in the future, or the patient may develop a new condition that would require a temporary acute-care hospital stay and transfer back to the nursing home, with Medicare-approved days resulting. A long-term stay may make the patient eligible for Medicaid benefits.

This approval also means that the facility has met federal standards and that you do not have to worry about checking on mundane items such as the administrator's current license, the fire emergency system or menu rotations.

These items, which are covered under federal guidelines, are enforced by state inspectors.

## STEP TWO: LOOK AT THE FACILITY'S LAST STATE NURSING HOME INSPECTION REPORT.

The nursing home administration is required to either post or have available their last inspection report. In all probability this report will indicate some deficiencies for even the best of facilities, and therefore must be read with a discerning eye. An uncovered dirty laundry basket, or a dishwasher two degrees below the water-heat standard, are typical examples of unimportant items. Repeated deficiencies for lack of adequate personnel, inadequate nursing care and bad diet are far more serious.

Utilizing some data compiled from these inspection reports, the federal government in 1988 and again in 1990 published a national survey. These multivolume reports purported to be a "consumer's guide" to properly rating nursing homes throughout the country. The survey covered only 32 performance areas and failed to discriminate major from minor deficiencies and therefore is very misleading. It is difficult to determine from these reports alone if a nursing home is good or substandard.

The purpose of reviewing these reports is to winnow from your list of consideration the obviously poor homes that are cited for multiple important deficiencies. A key item to look for in these reports are citations for inadequate nursing personnel on duty. Without sufficient staff, there is no question that patients will suffer some form of neglect.

## STEP THREE: CHECK THE HOUSEKEEPING.

Look at the general housekeeping and condition of the building as you would a motel or hotel. However, keep in mind that people live permanently in the building, many of whom are incontinent or bedridden. There may be a smell of urine in the air; the important consideration is whether the odor is a stale one of some duration, or a recent one that will soon be cleansed. A strong smell of disinfectant or deodorizer might be an attempt by a home with poor housekeeping to hide lingering odors.

## STEP FOUR: CHECK THE FOOD.

There is no question that well-balanced meals, attractively served, are of prime importance to anyone in any institution, including nursing homes. Check to see that in-season fruits and vegetables are included in the menu and that the meals are basically prepared from scratch rather than assembled from large institutional cans. Watch to see if the meal served agrees with the posted menu and that the menu cycle is at least two weeks in duration.

The main meal should be served at noon, with a lighter meal in the evening. Midday and evening snacks, with juice, should be provided. If a patient is unable to go to the dining room, check to see if the food is still warm when it arrives at the room. If a patient is unable to feed herself, does the nurse's aide patiently help with the eating process? Some elderly are slow eaters. Busy staff members may often be impatient and proceed at a pace too fast for the patient. A harried meal is not only inhospitable, but in the case of elderly with swallowing or other difficulties can cause aspiration of food particles into the lungs.

In some nursing homes aides simultaneously feed two or more patients. This has the advantage of efficiency when slow eaters are involved and also provides socialization. The authors have no quarrel with this procedure, and feel that it is far preferable to a harried feeding.

The type of food served should be appropriate for the elderly's ability to eat. A large steak might be enticing for a younger adult, while easy to cut and chew pot roast might be more practical for an older person with full dentures.

### STEP FIVE: OBSERVE PATIENT ACTIVITY.

It is convenient for nursing homes to let residents remain in their beds and not be ambulated and dressed. It is far easier to physically or chemically restrain confused patients than to care for them properly. It is far more efficient to brush a stroke victim's hair or button that last button rather than watch while they struggle with this now difficult task as they relearn the activities of daily living.

The poor nursing home will have far less patient activity than the better institution. In a good nursing home the patients will be up, dressed and groomed, and ambulated either with help or with a walker or wheelchair.

There is no question that patients who are up, dressed and ambulated will have a greater sense of emotional and physical well being.

### STEP SIX: OBSERVE THE STAFF'S RELATIONSHIP WITH THE RESIDENTS.

Observation of the nursing staff's interaction with the residents will reveal more about the nursing home than 50 inspection reports. The way the staff talks, touches and responds to patients will tell a great deal about the quality of care they will deliver.

### STEP SEVEN: SPEAK WITH THE UNIT CHARGE NURSE AND/OR THE DIRECTOR OF NURSING CONCERNING SPECIFIC FACILITY POLICIES THAT AFFECT YOUR PATIENT.

If your patient is bedridden and/or confused, you must establish the home's policies concerning bed sores (inexcusable) and chemical and physical restraints (should be rarely used). The ambulatory and continent patient who is restrained in a wheelchair will shortly become immobile and incontinent. The patient who is constantly "snowed" by tranquilizers or other drugs will eventually have dubious mental clarity and runs the risk of serious side effects. In almost all cases, the use of physical and chemical restraints in nursing homes is done for the convenience of the staff rather than for the benefit of the patient.

The topic of activities of daily living should also be discussed at this meeting. The medical condition of your patient will more specifically direct the course of this conversation and advice from the patient's primary care physician will be most helpful in establishing topics. The general guideline is that your patient should be as active as possible and should do as much for him- or herself as is feasible.

## STEP EIGHT: LOOK FOR COMPASSION OVER COST.

The more expensive nursing homes are not necessarily the best. The very quiet and serene nursing homes are certainly not the best. Often, the more expensive establishments attempt to create an aura of serenity and opulence. This results in pristine halls, lobbies and sitting areas, which have the quiet demeanor of a fine resort hotel. Actually, during daylight hours, the halls and common areas should be filled with patients provided with a range of ambulatory devices. These residents should have full run of the building and be able to view visitors with open curiosity. Administrations overly concerned with expensive new admissions do not wish their visitors overwhelmed by this initial exposure.

It should now be apparent that nursing home patient abuse is more likely to arise from neglect rather than overt cruelty. Patients are restrained because it is easier for the staff. They are not turned adequately at night and therefore develop bed sores. They are fed too quickly because the aide has many more feedings to perform that shift, and call bells are not answered promptly because the shift is short of personnel.

In 1990 nursing homes reported a national shortage of 19% in registered nurses, 18% in LPNs and a turnover rate that often exceeded 100% for nurses' aides. This personnel shortage is exacerbated by the extremely poor training many of these staff members have received in geriatric problems.

As a final hint for the nursing home choice: Find a small, pleasant nursing home with an adequate staff made up of happy, long-term employees.

# MONITORING THE PATIENT

Although the patient's advocate may have taken great care and time to select and investigate the nursing home, errors can be made. Often, poor nursing care will become apparent only after some time. Only careful observation after admission will reveal the true quality of the nursing home's care and the attitude of the personnel toward their patients. An alert advocate who is watchful and somewhat knowledgeable might also improve the care the staff renders that particular patient.

## CHECK ON

**Pressure and bed sores.** If these sores are allowed to fester they can have severe consequences for the patient. The patient's advocate should check the heels, hips and coccyx (tail bone) for the first signs of skin breakdown.

**The use of restraints.** If a patient has been restrained, either physically or chemically, immediately discuss this situation with the attending physician. Care should be taken to peek under lap blankets of wheelchair patients for the presence of restraints. If a patient seems drowsy, an inquiry should be made to find out if new medications have been authorized.

**Is the patient ambulated daily?** It is time consuming for the staff to ambulate the partially immobile patient. However, the benefits of this activity, both emotionally and physically, cannot be overemphasized.

**Be alert to changes in condition or treatment.** If any new drugs or therapies have been prescribed, or the patient seems to have changed, immediately discuss this with the medical staff.

**Check on roommates and call bells.** Disruptive or inappropriate roommates can be a serious problem. Circumstances may make it impossible to have a perfect personality pairing, and for some independent individuals, that may be impossible. Staff, family and patients must strive to make the most practical combinations work.

A poor or understaffed nursing home may go so far as to disconnect call bells or even ignore them. Unhappy patients may overutilize call bells by such maneuvers as asking for a pillow fluff while meals are being served. Call bells **must** never be disconnected, should be answered with dispatch, and patients should be considerate.

**Are the nursing and medical care plans followed?** Shortly after admission the nursing staff and patient's primary care physician prepared nursing and medical care plans. These documents addressed the patient's medical problems and outlined goals and treatments. Advocates must be aware of these plans and check to see if the suggested therapies are carried out.

## COMPLAINTS

Patient families and advocates will often respond to the unfamiliar nursing home situation and also attempt to relieve their guilt by aggressive verbal attacks on the staff. Unhappy patients, who would rather be home, exacerbate this situation with long lists of exaggerated complaints. Patients and families, fully aware of the huge sums of money they are spending for this care, may not understand why the resident's most frivolous needs are not taken care of immediately. This desire is in conflict with good nursing, which requires the patient to perform as many activities of daily living as she is capable of. Merge these factors together, mix with understaffed and overworked nursing home personnel, and a potential battlefield is created.

It is incumbent on the patient's advocate to understand these conflicting needs and desires and to discern which complaints are legitimate. Complaints should be initially directed to the unit's charge nurse. It is recommended that this conference not be attempted at the beginning or end of a shift, as this is the time for "report," the passing of important medical information from the outgoing to the new charge nurse. Complaints should be made in a positive manner, and sufficient time given for rectifying the problem.

If a problem cannot be resolved, or if it is of a serious nature, an approach should be made to the director of nursing, then the patient's attending physician and the nursing home administrator.

State Nursing Home Ombudsmen were established in every state by federal mandate. They have the power to enter any nursing home, examine records, take formal complaints and attempt to either resolve the problem or call in the necessary other state agencies that may be empowered to take action. The phone numbers for your ombudsman can be obtained through the local agency on aging or your state department of health or aging.

## PATIENT'S BILL OF RIGHTS

A copy of a nursing home patient's bill of rights is reproduced in the Appendix and should be read by anyone selecting a nursing home. There are several paragraphs in the "Payment for Services" section that require specific mention:

"You cannot be required to waive any rights you may have to receive Medicare or Medicaid . . ." Nursing homes receive a flat daily rate for Medicaid patients that is far below what private patients pay. Many facilities would like you to believe that if Medicaid benefits are applied for at any time in the future that a change of institutions is required. Unless the home is a nonapproved Medicare/Medicaid facility, this would be illegal.

"You cannot be required to have a third party guarantee payment for your care . . ." Nursing homes would often like all children and grandchildren as responsible parties, but this is now excluded. This provision does not preclude payment guarantees for *patient* funds, which may be administered by others such as in the case of powers of attorney, etc.

"You cannot be required to pay or give the facility any gift, money or donation for their consideration as a condition of admission . . ." This was a favorite tactic in the past that many nursing homes utilized when there was a long waiting list; it too is now illegal.

# IT MIGHT BE THE LAST STOP

A first visit even to a good nursing home by a relative of a prospective patient may be an overwhelming experience. The building may have unpleasant odors, and patients may wander the halls with various types of ambulatory devices, some perhaps speaking in an incomprehensible language. Other patients, observed through open room doors, may be bedridden or perhaps comatose. It can be a depressing experience, and yet from this experience a meaningful assessment of the institution must be made.

The selection of a nursing home is the most important single decision that can be made in the whole elderly housing continuum. The resident is not only physically and emotionally vulnerable, but usually unable to act independently. This dependence can cause even casual care to have a significant effect on the length and quality of life.

Beyond any doubt, the main criterion in the selection of a nursing home should be the quality of the floor nurses and their assistants. This quality far exceeds physical amenities, attractive menus or varied recreational programs.

The mediocre nursing home might have passive patient abuse through simple neglect. The excessive use of physical and chemical restraints and the failure to monitor delicate elderly skin conditions are the two primary areas of this neglect.

Nursing home costs are a problem that society must soon face. They are high, profits are low, and increased care is desired. The squeeze is obvious. Half of all patient charges are paid by the patient or her family. This often results in impoverishment and conversion to Medicaid, a welfare entitlement program. It has always seemed somewhat cruel to force middle-class individuals to liquidate their life savings until they meet Medicaid eligibility requirements. Private long-term-care insurance has attempted to fill the gap, but it is presently too expensive for most individuals except for a narrow age window.

Skilled nursing homes operate with a high occupancy rate, and therefore a hurried search is often a limited search. Anticipation of a possible future nursing home need allows time to make a proper search and arrange placement on a waiting list.

The families of potential nursing home patients must understand that often this alternative is not only a necessary alternative, but the best solution for the patient's needs. A thorough nursing home search with follow-up monitoring visits should do much to assuage any guilt felt over this type of placement.

# APPENDIX

## USEFUL ADDRESSES

### SENIOR ORGANIZATIONS

American Association of Retired Persons (AARP)
909 K Street N.W.
Washington, D.C. 20049
(202) 872-4880
A sophisticated organization that publishes many free pamphlets and brochures on subjects of interest to the retired. Its magazine *Modern Maturity* is provided with a yearly membership fee of $5. One of the best buys in town.

Gray Panthers
311 South Juniper St., Suite 601
Philadelphia, PA 19107
(215) 545-6555
An activist group to combat ageism. Many local chapters.

National Alliance for Senior Citizens
2525 Wilson Blvd.
Arlington, VA 22201
(703) 528-4380
Lobbies state and federal governments and publishes *Senior Guardian* monthly.

Older Woman's League
730 11th St. N.W., Suite 300
Washington, D.C. 20001
(202) 783-6686
An advocacy group that publishes *The Owl Observer*.

187

**Support Groups (Check for local chapters):**

Alzheimer's Association
70 East Lake St.
Chicago, IL 60601
(800) 621-0379

American Parkinson's Disease Association
116 John St.
New York, NY 10038
(212) 685-2741

National Association for the Deaf
814 Thayer Ave.
Silver Spring, MD 20910
(301) 587-1788

National Federation for the Blind
1800 Johnson St.
Baltimore, MD 21230
(301) 659-9314

National Multiple Sclerosis Society
205 East 42nd St.
New York, NY 10017
(212) 986-3240

**Groups with useful information for the retired:**

American Association of Homes for the Aging
1129 20th Street N.W., Suite 400
Washington, D.C. 20036
(202) 296-5960
Publishes a list of accredited life-care communities and a directory.

Elderhostel
75 Federal St.
Boston, MA 02110
(617) 426-8056
Offers short courses and room and board at more than 1,000 universities in the U.S. and abroad.

National Academy of Elder Law Attorneys, Inc.
1730 East River Rd.
Tucson, AZ 85718
(602) 881-4005
A professional organization of lawyers who specialize in legal problems of the elderly. Send a self-addressed, stamped envelope for the names of such lawyers in your area.

National Association for Home Care
519 C Street N.E., Stanton Park
Washington, D.C. 20002
(202) 547-7424
A professional organization that can provide information about home nursing care.

National Association of Residential Care Facilities
1205 West Main St., Room 209
Richmond, VA 23220
(804) 355-3265
This association of board-and-care facilities will provide a list for your state.

National Center for Home Equity Conversion
1210 E. College Dr., Suite 300
Marshall, MN 56258
(507) 532-3230
The experts on reverse mortgages. They will provide information about your area on request.

National Hospice Organization
1901 North Fort Meyer Dr.
Arlington, VA 22209
(703) 243 5900
This professional organization will provide a list of hospices in your area.

National Osteoporosis Foundation
1625 Eye St. N.W., Suite 822
Washington, D.C. 20006
(202) 223-2226
Send $1 for a 40-page booklet on this condition.

Shared Housing Resource Center
6344 Greene St.
Philadelphia, PA 19144
(215) 848-1220
This is the clearinghouse for match-up shared housing groups. They will provide a list of match-up programs in your area.

# STATES THAT REGULATE ADULT DAY CARE

**Standards for Certification Only**
Alabama
Colorado

Massachusetts
North Carolina
Rhode Island
South Dakota

**Standards for Funding Only**
Illinois
Michigan
Montana
New Hampshire
North Dakota
Washington

**Standards for licensing**
Arizona
Arkansas
California
Florida
Hawaii
Kentucky
Louisiana
Maine
Maryland
Minnesota
Missouri
Nebraska
Nevada
New Mexico
New Jersey
New York
Pennsylvania
South Carolina
Texas
Utah
Virginia
West Virginia

**Limited or no standards**
Alaska
Connecticut
Delaware
Georgia
Idaho
Indiana
Iowa

Kansas
Mississippi
Ohio
Oklahoma
Oregon
Tennessee
Vermont
Wisconsin
Wyoming

*Source: Intergovernmental Health Policy Project, Washington, D.C.*

# STATES WITH LIFE-CARE LAWS

Twenty-two states have enacted some sort of legislation to regulate life-care facilities (continuing care retirement communities):

| | |
|---|---|
| Arizona | Michigan |
| Arkansas | Minnesota |
| California | Missouri |
| Colorado | New Jersey |
| Connecticut | New Mexico |
| Florida | New York |
| Illinois | North Carolina |
| Indiana | Pennsylvania |
| Kansas | Texas |
| Louisiana | Virginia |
| Maryland | Wisconsin |

# BOARD-AND-CARE RESIDENTS' RIGHTS

The right to be accepted and treated as a resident; a resident may not be kept apart from other residents.

The right to reasonable privacy, including privacy of self and possessions, privacy in my room (or in my portion of the room) and privacy in personal affairs.

The right not to be physically or psychologically abused or punished by the operator, the operator's employees or family, other residents or any other person.

The right to live free from physical restraint, involuntary confinement and financial exploitation; the right to manage my own personal funds.

The right to full use of the facility, including freedom to use the living room, the dining room and recreation areas in compliance with the documented house rules; the right to voice grievances and recommend changes in policies and services.

The right to communicate privately by mail or telephone with anyone, including relatives, friends, caseworkers, medical and psychiatric facilities and members of public agencies; the right to reasonable use of the telephone in accordance with house rules.

The right to have visitors, provided the visits are conducted at reasonable hours and the visitors are not actively disruptive to the operator, the operator's employees or family or other residents.

The right to make visits outside the facility; however, there is a shared responsibility between the operator and me to make mutual arrangements for keeping in touch with each other.

The right to make my own decisions and choices in the management of my personal affairs in accordance with my abilities; the right to receive a response from the operator within a reasonable length of time when I make a request.

The right to expect the cooperation of the operator in achieving the maximum degree of benefit from my being a resident in the facility.

The right to exercise my choice to attend and to participate in religious activities.

Source: National Association of Residential Care Facilities

# A TYPICAL NURSING HOME
# PATIENTS' BILL OF RIGHTS

## EXERCISING YOUR RIGHTS

- You have the right to be fully informed, orally and in writing, in a language you understand, of your rights and the facility's rules governing resident conduct and responsibilities, and of changes in your rights and in the facility's rules.
- You have the right to exercise your rights as a resident and as a citizen. The facility must protect and promote your rights and encourage and assist you in exercising them.

- You have the right to be treated equally with other residents in receiving care and services, and regarding transfer and discharge, regardless of the source of payment for your care.
- You have the right to exercise your rights without fear of discrimination, restraint, interference, coercion or reprisal.

## DIGNITY AND SELF-DETERMINATION

- You have the right to be treated with consideration, respect and full recognition of your dignity and individuality.
- You have the right to reasonable accommodation of your individual needs and preferences, except when your health or safety or the health or safety of others would be endangered.
- You have the right to choose activities, schedules and health care consistent with your interests and your assessment and plan of care.
- You have the right to make choices about aspects of your life that are significant to you.
- You have the right to keep and use your personal possessions, as space permits, unless doing so would infringe on the rights, health or safety of other residents.
- You have the right to be notified before your roommate is changed.

## PRIVACY

- You have the right to privacy in accommodations, in receiving personal and medical care and treatment, written and telephone communications, in visits and in meeting with family and resident groups. However, the facility is not required to provide you with a private room.
- You have the right to associate and communicate privately with persons of your choice, including other residents.
- If married, you have the right to privacy for visits with your spouse.
- If you are married and your spouse is a resident of this facility, you have the right to share a room with your spouse, subject to his or her consent.

## COMMUNICATING WITH OTHERS

- You have the right to privacy in written and spoken communications.
- You have the right to send and receive unopened mail promptly.
- You have the right to have stationery, stamps and writing implements made available by the facility for you to purchase.
- You have the right to a regularly available telephone that you can use in privacy.
- You have the right to interact with persons both inside and outside of the facility.

- You have the right to receive information from agencies that act as client advocates and to have the opportunity to contact such agencies.

## VISITS

- You have the right to be visited by your family.
- You have the right to be visited by your attending physician, by the nursing home ombudsman, and representatives of federal and state agencies concerned with residential care.
- You have the right to be visited by any other person of your choice, including persons who provide services to nursing home residents, subject to reasonable restrictions.
- You have the right to refuse to receive any visitor you do not want to see.

## GROUP ACTIVITIES

- You have the right to participate in social, religious and community activities that do not interfere with the rights of other residents.
- You have the right to organize and participate in resident groups in the facility.
- Your family has the right to meet with the families of other residents in the facility.

## GRIEVANCES

- You have the right to voice grievances and recommend changes in facility policies and services to staff or to outside representatives of your choice.
- You have the right to have prompt efforts made by the facility to resolve grievances you may have, including those about the behavior of other residents.
- You have the right to file a complaint with the state Department of Health Services or the state Department on Aging regarding abuse, neglect or misappropriation of resident's property.

## CARE AND TREATMENT

- You have the right to choose your personal attending physician.
- You have the right to be fully informed, in a language you understand, about your total health status, including your medical conditions.
- You have the right to participate in planning your care and treatment and to be fully informed in advance about changes in your care and treatment that affect your well-being.
- You have the right to refuse treatment.

- You have the right to administer your own drugs, unless your care planning team has determined that it would not be safe for you to do so.
- You have the right to the opinions of two physicians concerning the need for surgery, prior to surgery, except in an emergency.
- You have the right to refuse to participate in experimental research.
- You have the right to be free from restraints and psychoactive drugs administered for discipline or convenience and not required to treat your medical symptoms. Physical and chemical restraints may be used only to ensure your physical safety or enable you to function better, and then only on the written order of a physician that states when and for how long they are to be used, except in an emergency.
- You have the right to have psychopharmacologic drugs administered only on orders of a physician, as part of a written care plan designed to eliminate or modify the symptoms the drug was prescribed to treat, and only if an independent external consultant reviews whether your drug plan is appropriate at least once a year.
- You have the right to be free from verbal, sexual, physical or mental abuse, corporal punishment and involuntary seclusion.
- You have the right not to perform work for the facility. If performing work for the facility is recommended as part of your care plan and suitable work is available, you have the right to choose to perform work for the facility and to choose whether you wish to work as a volunteer or for payment at prevailing rates, if your choice and the kind of work you will be doing are documented in your care plan.
- You have the right to see the results of current federal, state and local inspection reports and plans of correction.

## PERSONAL AND CLINICAL RECORDS

- You have the right to privacy and confidentiality of your personal records and clinical records.
- You have the right to approve or refuse the release of these records to anyone outside the facility, except when you are transferred to another health care institution or the release of your records is required by law or by third-party payors such as Medicare, Medicaid or private insurers.

## TRANSFER AND DISCHARGE

- You have the right to be allowed to stay in the facility and may not be discharged from the facility, except as provided by federal and state law. Federal and state law permit an involuntary transfer or discharge only when the transfer or discharge is necessary for your welfare and your welfare cannot be met in the facility; or transfer or discharge is appropriate because your health has improved so that you no longer need the services provided by the facility; or the health or safety of individuals in the facility is endangered; or, if you are paying for your care, your account is more than 15 days in arrears; or if the facility ceases to operate.

- You must be given 30 days' notice of a transfer or discharge from the facility unless the transfer or discharge is made because the health or safety of individuals in the facility is endangered; your health has improved sufficiently to allow for a more immediate transfer or discharge; immediate transfer or discharge is necessary because of an urgent medical need; or you have resided in the facility for less than 30 days. In such cases, you must be given as much notice as practicable.
- You have the right to appeal an involuntary transfer or discharge from the facility to the state Department of Health Services.
- You may be involuntarily transferred from one room to another within the facility only for medical reasons or for your welfare or that of other residents, as documented in your medical record. You must be given 30 days' written notice, except where the health, safety or welfare of other patients is endangered; where immediate transfer within the facility is required by your urgent medical needs; or you have resided in the facility for less than 30 days. In such cases, you must be given as much notice as practicable.
- You may not be involuntarily transferred or discharged from the facility or transferred within the facility if the transfer or discharge presents imminent danger of death.

## PAYMENT FOR SERVICES

- You have the right to be fully informed of the services available in the facility and, if you are paying for the cost of your care, of the per diem rate and charges for any services not covered by the per diem rate. If your care is paid for by Medicare or Medicaid, you have the right to be informed of the services that are not covered by Medicare or Medicaid and the charges for such services.
- You cannot be required to waive any rights you may have to receive Medicare or Medicaid, or to give assurances that you are not eligible for or will not apply for Medicare or Medicaid, as a condition of admission to or continued residence in the facility.
- You cannot be required to have a third party guarantee payment for your care as a condition of admission to or continued residence in the facility.
- You cannot be required to pay or give the facility any gift, money, donation or other consideration as a condition of admission to or continued residence in the facility.
- You have the right to be informed of how to apply for and use Medicare and Medicaid and how to receive refunds for previous payments covered by these programs.

## PERSONAL FUNDS

• You have the right to manage your personal financial affairs and cannot be required to deposit your personal funds with the facility.
• You have the right to have the facility manage your personal funds, if you authorize this in writing. You have the right to a quarterly accounting of your funds. A separate statement about how the facility manages residents' funds is provided.

I HEREBY ACKNOWLEDGE THAT I HAVE RECEIVED A COPY OF THIS NURSING HOME PATIENTS' BILL OF RIGHTS AND THAT IT HAS BEEN EXPLAINED TO ME BY THE STAFF.

_____
Signature of Resident
or

_____
Signature of Conservator,
Power of Attorney or Relative
(Please specify)

_____
Date

# LONG-TERM CARE INSURANCE CHECKLIST

Does the policy pay benefits for skilled, custodial and at-home care?

Must you be hospitalized before you receive benefits?

Does the policy provide coverage for senile dementia?

Does the company agree to renew as long as premiums are paid?

Is there an inflation rider?

Must you have skilled nursing care before you get benefits for custodial or home care?

Does the plan allow you to choose the amount of daily coverage?

Will the cost of coverage increase as you get older?

Will the policy cover you if you move to another area?

Does the company provide a case manager?

Will the premium always be based on your age at time of enrollment?

Is the company qualified to write this insurance in this state?

What is the waiting period for preexisting conditions?

What percentage of the skilled nursing home cost do they pay for? Custodial care? Home care?

What is their A. M. Best rating?

What is the yearly premium for an $80-a-day benefit, with a 90-day waiting period, an inflation rider, for a minimum of two years of coverage?

# GLOSSARY

**accessory apartment.** A separate and complete living unit within a private home.

**activities of daily living (ADLs).** Routine personal activities such as eating, grooming and dressing.

**acute-care hospital.** A general hospital able to provide full medical services.

**adult day care center.** A five-day-a-week program that offers health support, a noon meal, protective oversight and recreation for the impaired elderly.

**Alzheimer's disease.** A progressive and terminal dementia of unknown cause.

**assessment** (condominium). A unit owner's proportionate share of the annual budget or common charges for the maintenance of common areas and other expenses.

**assisted-living unit.** A small apartment that has full meal services, housekeeping and protective oversight available. Part-time nursing care might also be included.

**continuing-care retirement community (CCRC).** See **life-care community.**

**chronic disease.** A disease that is permanent and commonly disabling.

**common charges** (condominium). The popular term for the monthly proportionate share of the yearly budget for the common areas that are to be paid by each individual owner.

**condominium.** Form of property ownership in which units are individually owned and common property is owned jointly by all unit owners.

**condominium ownership.** Individual ownership of an apartment or town house, with shared ownership in the surrounding common areas.

**congregate housing.** Housing that offers individual apartments in a complex that provides some meals and other senior support services.

**cooperative ownership.** Occupancy of an apartment granted by virtue of ownership of shares in the corporation that owns the building.

**custodial care.** Room, board and protective oversight delivered on a long-term basis without routine medical and nursing services.

**diagnosis related group (DRG).** A grouping of various medical conditions for the purpose of paying an acute-care hospital a flat daily rate.

**domiciliary care.** Group living with a professional manager or administrator present.

**ECHO housing (Elder Cottage Housing Opportunity).** A small house for the elderly constructed or moved to the lot that contains another home, usually of the elder's family.

**first-generation elderly.** The recently retired.

**foster care.** A system in which nonrelated older persons live with a family that provides meals, housekeeping and personal care.

**frail elderly.** Those over 62 who need help with two or more activities of daily living.

**geriatric assessment center.** A specialized unit in a medical center that evaluates the physical and cognitive functions of an elderly person.

**group home.** A shared housing arrangement where ownership of the unit is not held by any single member of the group. They are often sponsored by public or philanthropic groups.

**home equity loan.** A second mortgage.

**home equity conversion loan.** See *reverse mortgage.*

**home health care agency.** A private or nonprofit company that delivers skilled nursing care and at least one other therapeutic service to the home.

**homemaker service.** A private or nonprofit company that provides nonmedical support in the home, such as food preparation, shopping, cleaning and grooming.

**hospice.** An organization that provides pain relief, emotional support and medical management for the terminally ill. The hospice group can operate either through home visits, its own facility, or as part of a nursing home or hospital.

**incontinence.** Involuntary loss of urine or feces.

**intermediate nursing home.** A facility for individuals who need some skilled nursing care but who are usually ambulatory, continent and not as frail as those in a skilled nursing home.

**licensed practical nurse (LPN).** A graduate of a state-approved LPN course, usually of a year's duration, that emphasizes clinical skills. LPNs are licensed by the state health department.

**life-care community (CCRC).** Congregate living for the elderly in which guaranteed access to a skilled nursing home is also provided.

**life expectancy.** The length of time one is projected to live.

**longevity.** The maximum life expectancy for a species.

**long-term care.** The medical and support services necessary for individuals with chronic illness or other conditions that will continue for an indefinite period. Long-term care can be either at home or in a medical facility.

**maintenance (co-operative).** The popular term for the building's common charges that are to be paid by the shareholders.

**Medicaid (Title 19).** A joint federal/state entitlement program that provides payment for medical costs for those who qualify financially.

**mobile (manufactured) homes.** Compact factory-assembled housing units.

**modular units.** A house or apartment that is constructed in sections, which are moved to the building's location for final assembly.

**morbidity.** The incidence of disease in a given group of individuals.

**mortality.** The incidence of death in a given group of individuals.

**multi-infarct dementia (MID).** A form of senile dementia caused by a series of small strokes.

**nonprofit facility.** An organization in which no earnings are distributed to anyone, but are returned to the facility.

**precut homes.** Housing units whose components are cut, finished and fabricated in a factory, but are assembled on the building lot.

**protective oversight (board-and-care or custodial homes).** Nonmedical supervision of residents with the primary purpose of keeping them from physical harm.

**registered nurse (RN).** A graduate of a state-approved nursing school, of from two to four years' duration, who has been licensed by the state.

**resident's council.** Elected members of the residents or patients in senior housing who meet on a regular basis to provide liaison with the administration.

**respite care.** Temporary alternative care for the frail elderly to provide rest for the primary caregiver.

**restraints, chemical.** Medications given for the purpose of inhibiting behavior or movement.

**restraints, physical.** A mechanical device used for the purpose of restricting movement.

**retirement counties.** Counties so designated by the U.S. Department of Agriculture if a recent population increase of at least 15% is attributable to elder migrations.

**reverse mortgage** (home equity conversion loan). A loan taken by a property owner against a portion of the home's equity. This loan is repaid after a specified number of years, when the property is sold or when the owner dies.

**second-generation elderly.** Those who have begun to experience the first debilitating effects of chronic illness, and who realize that their functions are declining because of aging.

**self-transfering.** The ability of an individual to move from bed to chair to commode or toilet and back again without assistance.

**shared home.** A living arrangement in which two or more individuals have separate bedrooms but who share the remainder of the dwelling.

**skilled nursing home.** A medical facility that is able to deliver around-the-clock skilled nursing care.

**supplemental security income (SSI).** A federal entitlement program, sometimes augmented by the state, that provides additional income for the aged and disabled with inadequate resources.

**third-generation elderly.** Those who need extensive assistance in routine activities of daily living.

# BIBLIOGRAPHY

Action for Older Persons, Inc. *Your Retirement—How to Plan for a Secure Future*. New York: Arco Publishing, 1984.

Carling, Vivian F., and Mansberg, Ruth. *Where Can Mom Live?* Lexington, Mass.: Lexington Books, 1987.

Commonwealth Fund. *Old, Alone and Poor*. New York: Commonwealth Fund, 1987.

Cooper, Marion, ed. *The World's Top Retirement Havens*. Baltimore: Agora Inc., 1986.

Dickenson, Peter A. *Sunbelt Retirement*. Glenview, Ill.: Scott Foresman and Company, 1986.

———*The Complete Retirement Planning Book*. New York: E. P. Dutton, 1984.

Dychtwald, Ken, and Flower, Joe. *Age Wave*. Los Angeles: Jeremy P. Tarcher, Inc., 1989.

Forrest, Mary; Forrest, Christopher; and Forrest, Richard. *Nursing Homes: The Complete Guide*. New York: Facts On File, 1990.

Gerber, Jerry; Wolff, Janet; Kloves, Walter; and Brown, Gene. *Lifetrends: The Future of Baby Boomers and Other Aging Americans*. New York: Stonesong Press (MacMillan), 1989.

Gold, Margaret T. *Guide to Housing Alternatives for Older Citizens*. Mt. Vernon, N.Y.: Consumers Union of the United States, 1985.

Howells, John. *Retirement Choices for the Time of Your Life*. San Francisco: Gateway Books, 1987.

Kane, Robert and Kane, Rosalie A. *A Will and a Way: What the United States Can Learn from Canada about Caring for the Elderly*. New York: Columbia University Press, 1985.

Medical Care and Research Foundation, Inc. *Providing New Directions, New Hope in Board and Care*. Denver: Medical Care and Research Foundation, 1988.
Newcomer, Robert; Lawton, Powell; and Byerts, Thomas, eds, *Housing an Aging Society*. New York: Van Nostrand, 1986.
Raper, Ann Trueblood, ed. *National Continuing Care Directory, 2nd Edition*. Des Plaines, Ill.: Scott Foresman and Company AARP Books, 1988.
*Retirement Directory*. Highland Park, Ill.: Woodall Publishing Company, 1986.
*Retirement Places Rated*. Rev. ed. Chicago: Rand McNally, 1990.
Savageau, David. *Retirement Places Rating Guide*. 3rd ed. New York: Prentice-Hall, 1990.
Smith, Wesley J. *The Senior Citizen's Handbook*. Los Angeles: Price, Stern, Sloan, Inc., 1989.
Sumichrast, Michael; Shafer, Ronald; and Sumichrast, Marika. *Where Will You Live Tomorrow?*. Homewood, Ill.: Dow-Jones Irwin, 1981.
Uris, Auren. *Over 50*. Radnor, Penn.: Chilton Book Co., 1979.
Walford, Roy L. *Maximum Life Span*. New York: W.W. Norton and Company, 1983.
Winkelvoss, H. E. and Powell, A.V. *Continuing Care Retirement Communities: An Empirical, Financial and Legal Analysis*. Philadelphia: University of Pennsylvania, 1984.

# ARTICLES AND PAMPHLETS

AARP. *The Board and Care System: A Regulatory Jungle*. Washington, D.C., AARP, 1989.
AARP. *Preserving Independence, Supporting Needs: The Role of Board and Care Homes*. Washington, D.C.: Public Policy Institute, AARP, 1989.
AARP and the Federal Trade Commission. *Your Home, Your Choice*. Washington, D.C.: AARP, 1989.
Cloud, Deborah A. ed. *The Continuing Care Retirement Community*. Washington, D.C.: American Association of Homes for the Aging, 1984.
*Consumer Reports*. "Communities for the Elderly," February 1990, pp. 123–131.
Connecticut Housing Finance Authority. *Reverse Annuity Mortgage Loan Program*. Hartford, 1989.
Continuing Care Accreditation Commission. *Accredited Continuing Care Retirement Communities*. Washington, D.C., 1989.
Hartford Insurance Group. "Hartford House." Hartford. 1990.
Hubbard, Linda, ed. *Housing Options for Older Americans*. Washington, D.C.: AARP, 1984.
Levites, Mitchel. "Homeless in America." *New York Times,* June 10, 1990.

Mitchel, John. "Life Care Services Reorganizes." In *Contemporary Long-Term Care,* June 1987.

National Association for Home Care. *Homecare.* Washington, D.C., n.d.

*NARCF Directory of Residential Care Facilities.* Richmond, Va. National Association of Residential Care Facilities, 1987.

*NARCF Informational Directory.* Richmond, Va.: National Association of Residential Care Facilities, 1989.

National Council on the Aging. *Perspective on Aging.* July-August 1988.

Pastalan, Leon A. "Retirement Communities." *Generations,* Summer 1985, pp. 25–28.

Pennsylvania Department of Aging. *Older Persons and their Homes: Today and Tomorrow.* (research monograph) Lehigh University, June 1986.

Somers, Ann R. "The Continuing Care Retirement Community: One Viable Option for Long-term Care," *DRG Monitor.* 6:4, Dec. 1988.

U.S. Department of Housing and Urban Development. *Section 202 Direct Loan Program for Housing for the Elderly or Handicapped—Processing Handbook.* Washington, D.C.: Government Printing Office, March 1983 and revised.

U.S. General Accounting Office. *Board and Care: Insufficient Assurances That Resident Needs Are Identified and Met.* Washington, D.C.: Government Printing Office, 1989.

U.S. House of Representatives, Select Committee on Aging. *Board and Care Homes in America: A National Tragedy.* Washington, D.C.: Government Printing Office, 1989.

# INDEX

## A

Abandonment (fear of), 107, 158, 176
Accelerated death benefit insurance policies, 175
Accessory apartments, 27, 28, 78-81, 86
Accidents, 22, 23, 26, 147, 177
Accountant (CPA), 58, 128, 137, 141
Activities of daily living (ADLs), 2, 6, 22, 23, 48, 89, 102, 134, 135, 157, 162, 163, 164, 177, 180, 181, 183
Actuarial planning (CCRC), 123, 127, 129, 136
Acute-care hospitalization, 3, 101, 106, 108, 136, 139, 167, 174
Acute-care hospitals, 148, 167, 168, 169
ADLs *See* Activities of daily living
Administrator, board and care, 146, 160; CCRC 100, 101, 133, 139; nursing homes, 172, 178, 183
Adult communities *See* Retirement communities
Adult day-care centers, 2, 71, 72-73, 189
Adult group homes *See* Board and care facilities
Advocate (patient or resident's), 158, 159, 163, 165, 178, 182, 183
Affinity groups (CCRC), 110, 114
A-frames, 41, 49
Aging, 6, 7, 22, 23
Agriculture, U.S. Department of, 33. *See also* FMHA
Alabama, 33
All-inclusive plan (CCRC), 101, 104, 116, 120, 140
Alone (single living), 5, 7, 77, 87
Alzheimer, Alois G., 6
Alzheimer's Association, 10, 71, 188
Alzheimer's disease (SDAT), 6, 10, 11, 14, 23, 72, 134, 168
Alzheimer's unit, 15, 145
Ambulation, 180, 182, 184

American Association of Homes for the Aging, 118, 119, 121, 130, 132, 188
American Association of Retired Persons (AARP), 4, 155, 187
American Association of Retired Persons Travel Department, 39
American Parkinson's Disease Association, 188
Appraisers, 52, 53
Area agency on aging, 29, 65, 90, 159, 183
"Are you O.K.?" (telephone reassurance program), 68
Arizona, 32, 40, 41, 61, 75, 109, 174
Arkansas, 33
Arthritis (rheumatoid), 7, 10, 87, 147
Assessment and care plan, 73
Assisted living, 1, 2, 7, 8, 32, 53, 60, 61, 64, 77, 78, 88, 91, 92, 93, 95, 100, 102, 111, 117, 121, 135, 136, 138, 140, 141, 143
Assisted living homes *See* Board and care facilities
Attending physician, 101, 168, 171, 182, 183
Attorney *See* Lawyer

## B

Balance sheet (CCRC), 113
Baptist Church, 108
Barclay House, 136
Barrier-free units *See* Assisted living
Barter services, 82
Bathrooms, 25, 28, 86, 161, 164
Bed sores, 134, 166, 177, 180, 181, 182
Beverley Enterprises, Inc., 172
Biano, David, 70
Board and care facilities, 71, 91, 143, 144, 145, 147, 148, 149
  costs, 151
  how to select, 158-163
  monitoring resident, 163-164
  national tragedy, 152-157
Board of Directors,
  board and care, 159
  condominium, 44, 45

cooperative, 44, 45, 120, 121
Boston, 66
Building codes, 49, 80, 81
Building permits, 35, 80, 81
Burr, Clinton, 55
Bush, President George, 89
Byron Park (CA), 33

## C

Cable TV, 46, 57, 88, 99, 137
California, 3, 32, 40, 41, 72, 75, 83, 91, 108, 125, 144, 153, 174
California Community Care Facilities *See* Board and care facilities
Call bells, 162, 164, 181, 182
Canada, 52, 69, 83, 144, 150, 168, 170, 173, 175
Cape May (NJ), 33
Carillion project, 40
Cars (driving), 17, 19, 67, 158
Caruso, Enrico, 63
Catastrophic illness (1988 amendment to Medicare), 4
Catholic Church, 41, 108
Centvil Corporation *See* Carillion project
Cerebrovascular accident *See* Stroke
Certificate of need, 104
Charge nurse, 171, 180, 183
Children, 5, 7, 18, 20, 21, 24, 28, 31, 32, 39, 43, 79, 80, 183
Chore service (chore aid), 21, 41, 56, 65, 69, 75, 79, 86, 117, 140
Chronic care facilities *See* Skilled nursing homes
Chronic disease (chronic conditions), 7, 17, 22, 48, 64, 77, 89, 147, 156, 159, 167, 178
Civil War, 2
Classic Residences *See* Hyatt Corporation
Clergy, 65, 108, 158
Cognitive functions, 14, 158
Colorado, 75
Common charges (assessments) *See* Condominiums
Commonwealth Fund, 5
Community Option Program (WI), 66, 75

207

## DATE DUE

| | | | |
|---|---|---|---|
| | | | |
| | | | |
| | | | |
| | | | |
| | | | |
| | | | |
| | | | |
| | | | |
| | | | |
| | | | |
| | | | |
| | | | |
| | | | |
| | | | |
| | | | |
| | | | |
| | | | |
| | | | |
| | | | |
| GAYLORD | | | PRINTED IN U.S.A. |